77 TALKS FOR CYBERSPACE KIDS

77 talks for Cyberspace Kids

*Messages from the Truth Zone
for 8–12s*

**Chris Chesterton
and David T. Ward**

MONARCH
BOOKS

Mill Hill, London & Grand Rapids, Michigan

First published by Monarch Books in the UK 2002,
Concorde House, Grenville Place,
Mill Hill, London, NW7 3SA.

Distributed by:
UK: STL, PO Box 300, Kingstown Broadway, Carlisle,
Cumbria CA3 0QS;
USA: Kregel Publications, PO Box 2607
Grand Rapids, Michigan 49501.

ISBN 1 85424 598 8

British Library Cataloguing Data
A catalogue record for this book is available
from the British Library.

Book design and production for the publishers by
Bookprint Creative Services
P.O. Box 827, BN21 3YJ, England.
Printed in Great Britain.

Contents

Acknowledgements

The authors would like to thank Sheila Chesterton, Peter Goodyear and Anna Gibbs for ideas which have been used in this volume. They would also like to express their gratitude to Sue Aldridge, Franck and Rebecca Fama, Tony and Georgina Clay, and David Lant for permission to use their true-life incidents and stories.

The illustrations are by Greg Clifton. Full-colour versions of the drawings can be found on the www.77talks.co.uk website. Greg is a freelance Christian artist and his contact details can also be found on the website.

Introduction

What is cyberspace?

Imagine you are on a space station located halfway to the moon. You move from a clear window that gives you a breathtaking view of planet earth to another that has special properties. This window makes electronic communication visible. The cloud-swirled, blue globe is now only just discernible beneath a deep golden glow, a shining mist that engulfs the planet and thins out way into deep space beyond us.

What you are seeing is the myriad of phone calls, text messages, e-mails, information and entertainment downloads, newsflashes, and TV and radio broadcasts that fill both the ether and a dense spider's web of land-lines. This is cyberspace.

Every person on the planet who has a mobile phone or an Internet-linked computer — and that includes the majority of children in the so-called developed world — has instant access to every other person. They are creating and re-creating that mist, moment by moment. In just a few years after the publication of this book in 2002, most people will probably carry a vidi-phone that enables them not just to talk to friends but to access and view an unlimited range of information, news and entertainment.

At the moment of writing, the space station is imaginary, the vidi-phone is being developed and tested, and cyberspace is a present reality. Those born since 1990 have been raised in that reality. They spend part of every day, not in the three-dimensional world of physical space, but in the electronic world of instant communication to anywhere. They are the free citizens of cyberspace.

The cyber revolution is changing the whole concept of the world we live in. For those of us born before it really took off, we may use its tools, but it is much harder to change our mind-set. In the 20th century, the church struggled to find its way and its voice in a world devoted to materialism. How will it cope with a world whose essential nature is *immaterial* — the world of cyberspace and virtual reality? How can we, the communicators of the church, find the language in which to speak to these young cybernauts?

Maybe we can find a clue if we take another trip off-world. This time we won't need a space station. We are going to join a band of angels who have just materialized a few thousand miles above earth's atmosphere. Seeing the earth through their eyes, we are surprised to find that it looks very much like it did through the special space station window. There is the same golden glow, the same sense of an intense field of communication surrounding the planet.

But this time it isn't electronic. This is the spiritual life and the prayers of every human being who is reaching out to the Creator. This is the glow of the kingdom of God.

So perhaps we are better prepared to talk to this generation than we think. Jesus came preaching the good news of the kingdom of the heavens, a kingdom which was at hand, within reach, as close as a whispered prayer. He used stories and illustrations from his time — parables — to shine light on aspects of that kingdom. The girl walking home from school talking to a friend on a mobile phone is literally holding a parable in her hand. This is just what the kingdom is like. She is better placed to understand it than the hard-nosed materialists of the mid-20th century.

This volume is the result of asking the Master to reveal more parables and metaphors from the world that today's children live in. Some of them are drawn from cyberspace itself, some from the three-dimensional world of the physical universe we live in. But although many of the metaphors are new, the truths they illustrate are firmly rooted in our biblical heritage.

Take these ideas and adapt them to your own circumstances. Many are suitable for use in all-age worship and we have found both children and adults responding equally enthusiastically. If a presentation has engaged children effectively, then a further brief thought may be added to give adults more to chew on without children getting restless. If you are talking in school, check whether you need to insert a judicious "I believe . . ." or "Christians believe . . ." to respect the fact that the children are there as a captive audience. On the whole, the pieces in this book ask for a more explicit Christian response than those in the companion volume, *77 Talks for 21st Century Kids*.

Research has shown that only one third of the population learn primarily through what they hear, so we must make every effort not to exclude the other two thirds who learn by seeing and doing. Involve the children themselves as much as possible and use as many visual elements as you can. Dress up and use drama. Do not be afraid of emotion. Anything of any significance to human beings carries an emotional charge. Music is a wonderful vehicle for emotion, so use background music, especially for the kind of closing reflections we often include here as SOMETHING TO THINK ABOUT. Be sensitive to the response of your audience and, when appropriate, allow a time for music to continue or for silence, in order to give space for thought and private prayer.

Below are some further thoughts on the cyberspace generation and how to connect with them. But technology is changing fast, so read newspaper and magazine articles to keep abreast. Find out how the children themselves respond to this technology and use it. At the same time, be aware of the other human needs which are often unmet in children's lives and which may be the ground on which we in the church can meet them and create relationships. And may those relationships be a key factor in many children becoming as "at home" with prayer to their Creator as they are with conversation through their mobile phones.

Five keys to understanding cyberspace kids

KEY 1: I WANNABE A CELEBRITY

Back in the 1960s, Andy Warhol said, "In the future everyone will be famous for fifteen minutes." Warhol's future is now.

Today's "royals" are the personalities created by the media and sports industries. Many children aspire to join them. And fifteen minutes — or, at least, fifteen seconds — of TV fame has never been easier to achieve. You can apply to get on a quiz game or a reality show; you can raise money for one of the big TV charity nights; you can join a protest or a blockade. Beyond the limit, you can even go out and shoot fellow schoolkids.

If you have the right sort of face or personality or skills, you can make it. But that brings with it the fear of being excluded, of being a nobody. It narrows the horizons and devalues the gifts and qualities of the majority of "ordinary" people.

How do we respond to the instant fame culture? How do we interact with our young celebrity wannabes, their hopes and their fears?

In considering our response to each of these keys to understanding cyberspace kids, we take our cue from the counsel of Jesus to be **"in the world, but not of the world"**. There are ways in which, with scriptural integrity, we can "go with the flow" and recognize God-given impulses and needs. But equally, to be true to the revelation we have been given, we have to take a stand and declare truths which are counter-culture. As we do the former, we gain a hearing for the latter.

Going with the flow

Jesus took children on his knee and blessed them when the disciples were trying to shoo them away. At Passover, Jewish children have a central place, finding the hidden bread and asking, "Why is this night special above all nights?"

Knowing the unique value that God places on every individual, we can seek ways to make children feel special. We can examine our church services and find ways to include children in active roles. We can bring them out to take part in the message — as in many of the talks in this book — and applaud them for doing so. We can ask them to prepare sketches or prayers or artwork. We can celebrate their achievements, including secular things like being part of sports teams or passing exams. This also underlines that Christianity is part of everyday life and not just for Sundays.

Taking a stand

The virtue of humility, of deliberately choosing **"to take the lowest place"**, is totally alien to our celebrity culture. We can only start by directing children's eyes to the greatness of God the Creator. This is where talks like "Cataclysmic love" and "10,000 trillion stars" are important. As children begin to appreciate the awesome power of the Creator, they can start to see themselves as they really are.

Then we shall want to help our children to see Jesus as the greatest man who ever lived, besides whom all our celebrities fade into shadows. And this extraordinary man and incomparable teacher is our best friend! But here we have a problem. The 20th century church largely lost contact with the Jesus of the gospels and could only see the Christ of the epistles.

So we pay lip-service to the Sermon on the Mount, but rarely preach on it. And the houses built on rock and sand, or Jesus' encounter with Zacchaeus, are good for bouncy kiddies' songs but seem to have no relevance for grown-ups. It is no wonder that young people turn their backs on the church when the adults in the pews and pulpits pay so little regard to the acts and words of the Master they claim to follow! Before we speak to children, we need prayerfully to ask Jesus to open our own eyes to see him as he is. If we are to take a stand against the culture of the world, we need first to take a stand against the culture of the church.

KEY 2: LIVING IN CYBERSPACE

To an ever-increasing extent, a child can live in the web of relationships he or she chooses. You no longer either walk home alone or in the company of a classmate (if you walk at all) — you switch on your mobile and walk home in the company of the friend of your choice.

At home, you log into a chat room on the computer. You are now part of a group whose members may be in the USA or Korea or Argentina. Geography and physical distance have no meaning. You no longer inhabit body-space, but cyberspace. Very shortly, even language barriers will have disappeared as translation software allows instant communication.

This accelerates the trend for social groupings to be less and less constrained by the place in which people live. The child whose passion is a particular form of computer gaming or music finds like-minded people on the web. The outsider in the classroom becomes an insider in an online community of soul mates. The disabled child finds others with a similar condition whom she can share her feelings with, or else enters a world of freedom where physical attributes have no meaning at all.

Going with the flow

In the introduction we touch on the images that cyberspace gives us: the worldwide web of prayer, instant communication with God, sharing intimately with the friend you cannot see. These are the kind of parables that are developed throughout this book.

When we think about the possibilities that are opened up to the lonely or to those with unusual medical conditions, for example, we realize the value of cyber community to minorities and the marginalized. One columnist said this about Silicon Valley: "It's about kids who couldn't walk down the hall in high school without being beaten up or insulted. Nerdy and reclusive kids who are nevertheless yanking the rug out from under 21st century civilization."[1] Does that have echoes of the Old Testament prophets or the early church? Maybe Elijah would not have thought he was the only one not to have bowed the knee to Baal if he had had access to the Internet! Cyberspace technology is just as powerful a tool for good or for evil as the printing press. It is up to us to push the good for all we are worth.

Taking a stand

"The Word became flesh and made his dwelling among us. We have seen his glory." The immaterial became material. The beyond-space became space-bound, wrapped in three dimensions tighter than any swaddling bands.

The incarnation teaches us the immense premium God places on meeting us "in the flesh". He knows our needs. When we relate to children through midweek groups or uniformed organizations or more informal contacts, we continue and extend what God did in Jesus. Stories of how children respond to things like table games and dressing-up show that we do not need to be ashamed of offering "old-fashioned" activities. Indeed, the more children become immersed in cyberspace, the more they will need and welcome direct human contact. A pendulum swing back to valuing such opportunities may not be far off.

KEY 3: LIMITLESS CHOICE

Hundreds of TV channels, music of any kind to download onto your personal player, vast online libraries of films . . . choice is exploding. In education, it is no longer necessary to follow the teacher or textbook from A to Z. You pick your package, decide how you want to use it, begin at P, jump to F, check out how that relates to X, and finish your session with an Internet link that was updated just hours ago.

Because there are endless different groups of like-minded people online, you do not have to wear the same clothes or listen to the same music as the other kids in the neighbourhood to feel part of an "in" crowd. You can choose which particular crowd you want to be part of. It is not surprising that a "pick-and-mix" spirituality has become enormously popular, too.

Now think what it feels like to come from a world that offers choice on that scale to the kind of set programmes we lay on in church. For some, it feels like an intolerable restraint. For others, it is a relief to have someone else take the responsibility of choice off their shoulders. But that has its own dangers.

Going with the flow

Choice is one of God's fundamental gifts to humanity. In Genesis 2, Adam is given the choice of eating the fruits of any of the trees in the garden — except one. He is also given the task of choosing names for all the animals and birds. Within the limitations of our resources, we need to look for ways to offer choices to the children in our care.

Following teaching with the options of creating a drama, artwork, or a word-based activity (poem or story) not only gives children that choice but it allows them to use their own preferred learning style. We can restructure our children's programmes to give them that sort of choice.

One of the most important things we shall want to do with our children today is to help them learn how to choose wisely, as in "Dangerous attachments" or "Are we blind?" That means teaching them to think for themselves and allowing them to make some of their own moral choices. That may seem risky, but it was the risk God took with Adam and Eve in the garden.

Taking a stand

God gives us choice, lots of choice. But some of those choices are wrong. There is absolute truth and absolute morality. That runs entirely counter to today's hedonistic and libertarian society. Telling children that something is wrong cuts very little ice unless they have learned to trust and respect us. We need to give reasons, tell true-life stories that show the results of certain actions, accentuate the wonderful benefits of listening to conscience or to the wisdom of God in the Bible. Pieces like "Robots don't win prizes" and "Some adults never live" highlight some of those benefits.

KEY 4: COMMUNICATION IS VISUAL

Our window on the world is now the screen, from the giant cinema screen to the $6cm^2$ of the mobile phone. Communication is primarily visual. It is colourful, it moves fast, it has an excitement factor that the everyday world rarely has, and it is increasingly interactive.

A futher key factor about this visual world is that it communicates through stories. In Britain, the majority of TV ads don't say much at all about the product. Instead they place the product in the context of a 30-second story told in a sequence of very rapid images. Children are highly adept at decoding these stories and get the point — often humorous — much more quickly than adults. It is hardly surprising that sitting through a fifteen-minute sermon does not rate too highly on children's wish lists!

Going with the flow

God puts a rainbow in the sky, attracts Moses's attention through a burning bush, and prepares his people to understand salvation through the story of Passover with all its visual and sensory aids. The psalm-writers and prophets can barely open their mouths without images spilling out, and Jesus never spoke to the crowds without using parables. Have you noticed those two-sentence story-line ads for the kingdom that Jesus keeps slipping in? "The kingdom of heaven is like treasure hidden in a field . . ."

With a Bible full of such examples in our hands, we should be rejoicing that cyberspace kids are forcing us to go back to our roots. If your message isn't visual or interactive, or if it doesn't feature a story — bin it and start again. And do check out the www.77talks.co.uk website for photographs and artwork all ready for you to print and use.

Taking a stand

How much of the latest blockbuster movie you saw was real and how much of it was created inside a computer? The art of illusion is constantly reaching dazzling new levels of mastery — and we love it!

There is nothing wrong in this. Our imagination and technical skills are God-given abilities. The dangers lie in losing sight of the real world and in images that are deliberately manipulated in order to deceive. Once again, teaching children to think for themselves and to evaluate what they see is so important.

Illustrations from the cinema and TV are generally too ephemeral to be included in a book of this kind, but that is the only reason for their absence. We should seek to include them in our messages, but always draw our audience back to the world of real people, real pain, real joy, and the real wonders of a life infused by a supernatural God.

KEY 5: WE'RE SEVEN YEARS OLD — WE DON'T PLAY WITH TOYS

That is a quote from a documentary entitled *Getting Older Younger*. It looked at childhood through the eyes and with the tools of modern marketing. There were some sobering images, such as a group of toddlers, some barely out of nappies, who could not only instantly shout the names of products whose logos were shown to them, but could recognize them backwards through the thickness of the paper before it was turned round!

One of the findings was that Britain has an unenviable lead in the world: nowhere do children stop playing with toys younger than here. The seven-year-olds quoted above were into fashion clothes and make-up. Yet if they are just given the excuse that adults are into something, then kids will enthusiastically take up a toy and express their unfulfilled need to play. That explains why 2001 saw hulking teenage lads pushing themselves along the pavements on ridiculously undersized scooters!

Another of its findings was that children's favourite TV programmes are not those specially made for them, but soap operas. Previous generations learned about the adult world through hearing the gossip of their parents around the table and over the garden fence. Our children learn what it means to be grown up through their daily diet of soaps.

Going with the flow

Knowing how children view themselves helps us avoid the trap of talking down to them. None of the illustrations used in the talks in this book is particularly childish. That is why they can be used effectively in all-age worship. When we look at the ministry of Jesus, we see that he rarely, if ever, addressed himself directly to children. Yet references to them make it clear that they were part of the crowds who followed him. That simply underlines the fact that parables — stories and images — speak to people of whatever age.

As for soaps, some of us love them, some of us hate them. Either way, what we need to see is that they provide the meeting ground where we can engage with children and talk about their perceptions of the world. TV soap may be super-concentrated, but lurching from crisis to crisis, relationship to relationship, is exactly the way many people live. Let's come at this from a biblical perspective.

Taking a stand

Did Jesus have anything to say about soaps? Yes, a lot. The Sermon on the Mount is all about the kind of day-to-day community relationships that are portrayed in soap operas. (The exception is the discussion of the public aspects of religious practice which are part of most societies but not of most Western countries today.)

Look at how angrily people speak to each other in some soaps and with what contempt. That is where Jesus starts in his discourse. Adultery, divorce, disputes, money, stress and anxiety, blame and condemnation, dangerous friends — it is all there in Jesus' teaching. And his answer is not (as sometimes portrayed) to give us a new and impossibly difficult "law" to keep, but to tell us that an inner life of relationship to the Father and obedience to the Son is the only thing that can keep us whole in the struggles of day-to-day living. That must be the good news for today's cyberspace kids!

Aspects of this good news are brought out in many of the pieces in this book, but to really rediscover the relevance of the beatitudes and Sermon on the Mount we urge you to read *The Divine Conspiracy* by Dallas Willard.[2]

To quote from Willard's own introduction: "[Jesus] comes where we are, and he brings us the life we hunger for. As an early report reads, 'Life was in him, life that made sense of human existence' (John 1:4). To be the light of life, and to deliver God's life to women and men where they are and as they are, is the secret of the enduring relevance of Jesus. Suddenly they are flying right-side up, in a world that makes sense."[3]

To which we would simply add: Jesus comes to deliver God's life to the women and men *whom our precious cyberspace kids are rapidly becoming.*

NOTES
1 Chris Gulker, article in *The Independent*, 14 February 2002.
2 Dallas Willard, *The Divine Conspiracy* (Fount Paperbacks, 1998).
3 *Ibid.* p. 20.

Using the
www.77talks.co.uk
website

One of the most aggravating things authors of this kind of book sometimes do is to tell the reader to find a picture of something as an illustration. You can then spend hours searching through magazines, often in vain. To simplify your task, and to give added impact to your presentations, we have provided resources at our website, www.77talks.co.uk. These include photographs and cartoon drawings which you can print onto overhead projector (OHP) transparencies, the text of sketches ready to print out, and take-home artwork for the Christmas Watchers series. There is advice on printing for those unfamiliar with producing OHP transparencies at home.

In addition, there is a section devoted to artwork to accompany the companion volume, *77 Talks for 21st Century Kids*, plus links to other useful websites. You can also send in your own ideas on how you have adapted talks in the book or found an up-to-the-minute illustration.

You will find reference to these resources scattered throughout the book, but do check the website to see if others have been added.

Parables from Cyberspace and Deep Space

New ways of picturing truths for all time

1
Cataclysmic love

Theme

The origins of gold in colliding stars speaks to us of the power of God's unfailing love.

You will need

- gold jewellery, especially a wedding ring. If using this in a church, ask people in advance to bring something made of gold with them. You can then get them to hold it for the climax of the message.

Presentation

Show some jewellery and talk about it, especially any presents. The children may be able to tell you about something they have.

For some people, the most precious thing they have is their wedding ring. Wedding rings are nearly always made of gold. They symbolize the love two people have for each other and their promises to stick with each other through thick and thin for the rest of their lives.

Gold has always been much sought after and, for centuries, alchemists tried to discover how to turn base metals, such as lead or copper, into gold. They could never suspect that it would take a furnace heated to a billion degrees and the risk of being sucked into a black hole!

A physicist at the University of Leicester, Stephen Rosswog, solved the mystery of how gold is created with the use of a tool the old alchemists could not have dreamed of — a supercomputer. The theory is that all it needs is a couple of neutron stars colliding. A neutron star is the core of a burned-out star that was once like our sun, but which has collapsed into an incredibly dense state. A mass a million times heavier than the earth is squeezed into a ball just 20 kilometres (12.4 miles) across!

Iron into gold

If two neutron stars are close enough to attract each other by their powerful gravity, they spiral ever closer together until there is a cataclysmic collision releasing vast amounts of energy. The extraordinary forces involved change elements such as iron into gold and platinum. Huge amounts of these precious metals are thrown into space and become part of the dust clouds which in future eons will be the birthplace of new stars — and planets such as ours.

Who would have thought that the gold in a wedding ring — a symbol of peace, harmony and love — should have been created in a furnace of such unbelievable forces?

Perhaps we can see in that a picture of our whole world. Here we are on a piece of rock whirling through space. A few miles above us is the cold and vacuum of space that would kill us instantly. Seven light-minutes away is a nuclear furnace — our sun — with temperatures of 15 million degrees Celsius at its centre and a million degrees in the corona that surrounds it.

Temporary place

Our world is really only a fragile biosphere that is just a thin envelope stretched around the planet. The world seems huge to us, but in the vastness of space it is incredibly tiny. As far as we know, it may be the only place that can support life in the whole universe.

The nature of the Creator who made this is love. The Bible puts it very simply: **"God is love."** (1 John 4:16) That love is seen and demonstrated most wonderfully in Jesus. In love God used all the massive and violent forces of nature to create a fragile and temporary place for us to live in — the earth. A place not just to live, but to grow and think and discover — and learn to love ourselves. As that same part of the Bible goes on to say, **"We love because he first loved us."** (1 John 4:19)

Of course, human love is not perfect, and sometimes, sadly, it fails. But the love of God never fails.

Something to think about

If you have arranged for the group to bring something made of gold with them, get them to hold it now. Otherwise, get one child to come and hold something you have brought. Play some appropriate music and lead a quiet reflection like this:

When you hold a gold necklace, or chain, or ring that someone has given you because they love you, you can say to yourself,

> **This gold was formed in a billion degree furnace as stars collided, before the earth and sun even existed. It speaks to me of the immense power of the Creator who made all things. And the love of the person who gave it to me reminds me of the eternal love of that same incredible God who first loved us. Just as this gold will never rust, never tarnish, so God's perfect love will never fail me.**

2
Playing God
with E-Dog

Theme

A lesson on God's care for us from an electronic pet.

You will need

- to get a child to bring an electronic or cyber pet (the appearance and sophistication of these is developing all the time), especially one that complains when it gets hungry and can get sick or "die" if not cared for properly.
- Alternatively, use the picture of Pootch from *www.77talks.co.uk*.

Presentation

Get the children to talk about any electronic pets they have and what they have to do to look after them. Some of the children may have quite expensive toys, others pocket games or a "pet" that lives in a computer.

What can you learn from looking after a cyber pet? Well, it could teach you a lot about caring, for instance, that caring is not a quick one-off. Caring for a pet — or a person — is a long-term commitment.

Caring is not something you do when you want to do it, but when the pet — or person — needs it. If your pet gets sick and you neglect him, he'll die.

Caring means being responsible. You have to be there yourself or else arrange with someone else to take over when you can't be there.

Caring means doing unpleasant things sometimes, like cleaning up the mess.

Rewarding but sad

Caring isn't just being soft. Sometimes you have to say that something is wrong and reinforce that with discipline.

Caring can be very rewarding, but it can also be sad. People have been known to get genuinely upset and cry when they see a digital gravestone on a computer screen.

Something to think about

If you learn those lessons, you can learn something else, too. When you learn what it means to care, you can turn it round and appreciate God's love and care for you. Talking to parents one day, Jesus put it like this:

> **If your child asks for bread, do you trick him with sawdust? If he asks for fish, do you scare him with a live snake on his plate? As bad as you are, you wouldn't think of doing such a thing. You're at least decent to your own children. So don't you think the God who conceived you in love will be even better?**
> *Matthew 7:9–11*, The Message

If Jesus were around today, perhaps he would say something like this:

> **Learn a lesson from your electronic pet. If you take such good care of a virtual pet who only "lives" in a computer chip, how much more does God care for you, his real, live, flesh-and-blood creation!**

3
CD-ROM

Theme

**CD-ROMs and their contents give insights into Jesus'
statement that he is "the light of the world".**

You will need

- a spare or old CD-ROM or DVD.
- If you have several, you could write the letters L I G H T on
  them and hang them up as a mobile.

Presentation

We all know what this is — a CD-ROM. But imagine you
knew nothing about computers and had never seen one
before. Would you have any idea what to do with it? Use it
as a mirror, perhaps? Or a bird-scarer?

You know that this has an amazing amount of information
stored on it. It could be music, or photos, or a whole
encyclopaedia, or a computer game.

Can anyone tell us how all that information is stored on
this disc and how the computer reads it? . . .

Digital information is stored in the form of tiny pits on a
layer of the disk. The CD-ROM drive on your computer
uses a low-power laser beam to read the data. A laser emits
a beam of a special kind of light, light of a single colour in
which the light waves are all in step with each other. Laser
light provides a very powerful and fast means of reading
and transferring data.

One time, Jesus was speaking to people and he said,

I am the light of the world. The person who follows me will never live in darkness. He will have the light that gives life.   *John 8:12*

The **"light that gives life"** must be a very special sort of light. It must have a very special sort of power. How can we understand it? Does thinking about a CD-ROM give us any clues? Maybe it does.

My CD-ROM may contain pictures. The laser allows me to view them. Jesus was constantly putting pictures into the minds of his followers. Things like: **"A man was digging up a field when he found some treasure . . ."** or, **"A foolish man built his house on sand."** These pictures stick in people's memories. They help us understand what the world is really like, especially the way God sees it. So Jesus was taking data from God — information about the world and people as God created them — and transferring it to our minds in a way we can easily understand, just as we quickly take in the information in a picture when it comes up on the computer screen.

A glimpse of heaven

My CD may have songs or music on it. As far as we know, Jesus didn't write music. But all through the centuries ever since, his life has been the most amazing source of inspiration to musicians. Countless thousands of songs and hymns, as well as some of the greatest pieces of music ever written, were inspired by Jesus. This music can have the power to lift people out of their everyday lives and give them a glimpse of heaven.

My CD-ROM may contain fascinating and useful information about something I am interested in. It can teach me something I would like to learn. The teaching of Jesus has helped millions of people to live in a way that is right and good. It has inspired countless people to strive to make the world a better place.

33

What about computer games? Lots of computer games involve some sort of fighting. Surely Jesus wasn't into that! Well, playing is about preparing for real-life situations. And Jesus was quite clear that we are in a real-life battle — a battle between good and evil. From time to time he talked about the enemy — the devil, or Satan. Parts of the last book in the Bible, Revelation, almost read like the script for a computer game involving the defeat of Satan! Learning God's way of fighting that battle is one of the most important things we can do.

Something to think about

Some people learn a little about Jesus, but they don't understand what the fuss is about and the light just scares them away. Others look more closely. They discover that the more they know about Jesus, the more they understand and appreciate the world and themselves. They find that Jesus truly is **"the light that gives life"**.

4
Text test

Theme

We can see God in Jesus — when we learn to read the message.

You will need

- at least two mobile phones per team, so ask your group in advance to bring them.
- identical sets of four or five cards with Bible texts on them for each team.

Presentation

Divide your group into two or more teams and split each team into two halves. Get the team halves to swap phone numbers. Send one half of each team to the opposite end of the hall or to a different room. (It can be fun to have an adults-only team. They will be hopeless!) The aim is for the "home" group to send a Bible text (given to them on a card) as a text message to the "away" half of their team who must then write it down in full. (Minor spelling errors permitted!) The away group sends the message back to the leader in old-fashioned style — on paper carried by a runner. If the wording is correct, the next card is given to the home group. One of the verses to be sent is, **"Anyone who has seen me has seen the Father."** (John 14:9)

Award a prize to the team that completes the task in the shortest time.

Bring the groups back together and get one or two children to show how they condensed the Bible texts into mobile "text" to send them quickly. (This could be an educational experience for the adults.)

35

God wanted to send a message to the world to show people what he was like. But God is infinitely great. It is a bit like you trying to explain what and who you are to an ant. Impossible! So how could God do it? He sent Jesus. Jesus is God "condensed" into human form. But Jesus said, **"Anyone who has seen me has seen the Father."** Of course, it takes a bit of practice to see the all-powerful God, Creator of the universe, in Jesus, just as many adults have a job getting the message if you text it to them. You have to take the time to get to know Jesus so that you can see God in him. But it is worth the effort.

"Anyone who has seen me has seen the Father." Get the message?

A prayer

You could ask the group — or one or two in advance — to write prayers in text message format. These might be read from an overhead projector (OHP).

NOTE

If you can't run this as a team game (e.g. if you have a large group or are in school) try it as a game with one or two people at the front communicating to one or two at the back. Two messages will be enough.

5
Dangerous attachments

Theme

Exercising caution before we take someone as our hero or role model.

You will need

- two people to prepare a mime as follows:
  Number one mimes getting into a car, driving, parking, getting out, putting a coin into a supermarket trolley, collecting goods, paying, taking the goods back to the car, and driving off.
  Number two mimes getting into a car, driving, parking, getting out, putting a credit-card into a lock to force entry into a house, collecting items and putting them into a bag, exiting via a window, getting back into the car and driving off.

Presentation

Ask the group to watch the two mimes. Then ask them to guess what was happening in each. Give clues as necessary and perhaps re-run the mimes or parts of them.

One of the main ways we learn is by watching and copying. Much of what a baby learns comes from watching and listening to its parents — and brothers and sisters — and copying them. As we get older we discover that there are some things it is better not to copy, as when we see someone get into trouble for what they did.

We may also have a hero, or a role model — someone we look up to and want to be like.

As in the two mimes, it is not always easy at first to know

whether someone is a good model to follow. Will they help us to learn new things, to grow up, to become wiser — or will they lead us into things that may be harmful? How do we know?

In the famous "Sermon on the Mount", Jesus gave a warning about people who set themselves up as leaders and role models but who were actually quite dangerous people to follow. He said, **"By their fruit you will recognize them."** (Matthew 7:16, *New International Version*) What did he mean?

If Jesus was talking to people today, he might put it something like this:

> **Suppose you get an e-mail from someone with an attachment with a fun-sounding title. But when you open it, it contains a virus which crashes your computer. You know then that that person is not to be trusted. You have recognized the kind of person they are by the things that they do.**

Sound advice

So Jesus was giving some sound advice in the Sermon on the Mount. Be cautious, he was saying. Don't rush into trusting someone and following them before you have found out what they are really like. Look for the "fruit" — or the e-mail attachments — the effect they actually have in the world and on the people around them. Then you will know whether they are worth copying or not.

Sometimes it is the people who seem to be the most successful and have the most friends who are actually quite dangerous. They are usually very good at conning people. Every so often there is a story about someone like that in the news — a Robert Maxwell or a Jeffrey Archer. They end up disgraced or in prison — or even committing suicide. Jesus put it like this:

Every tree that does not bear good fruit is cut down and thrown into the fire. *Matthew 7:19*

They come to a sticky end.

When that happens to someone famous, his or her friends and followers feel pretty stupid. Everyone can see that they got taken in. They want to crawl away and hide under a stone.

So take your time in deciding who you can trust, which is a good gang to belong to, who is a hero worth following. It's better not to be one of the in-crowd now than end up with egg on your face later.

A prayer

Our Father in heaven, we've learned to be cautious about opening e-mail attachments without checking first. Teach us to be cautious about following other people. You know what every person is really like inside. When we meet someone who could be a dangerous person to get close to, speak to our spirits and help us to listen to that still, small voice inside. Amen.

6
One touch is all you need

Theme

Jesus used touch as a way of demonstrating the message of God's love.

You will need

- a digital watch if you have one.

Presentation

We are going to fast-forward to a morning in school a few years in the future. I am the teacher. You have done your homework — I hope! — and I am going to collect it in. If you people on the front row would just hold a finger up in the air like this . . . and I'll collect in your work. [Look at your watch — press a button on it if it is a digital watch — then touch each person's finger for one second.] Yes . . . thank you. Next . . . thank you . . . etc.

Now I'll take your work to my office and transfer it to my computer ready for marking. I set my wrist-unit . . . then place my finger on a touch-sensitive pad for a few seconds . . . That's it: a whole set of homework waiting to be marked!

How does it work? A research team at IBM in California calls this a Personal Area Network — or PAN for short. It allows information to be passed from one person to another simply by touch.

Transfer via bald spot

If you were wearing a PAN transmitter it would create a tiny electrical current over the surface of your skin — just 1 billionth of an amp. All you need to do is to touch my finger — or my nose — or even my bald spot! — and your essay, drawing, or whatever else you have prepared on your home computer, will be transferred to my PAN receiver.

It is absolutely safe; even combing your hair creates an electrical field 1,000 times greater. Handing in your homework will be completely painless! (Of course, teachers might get a shock if certain people handed in their homework on time!)

That might be a few years away, but touch is now — and always has been — a vital way of people communicating with each other. Touch gives us messages we all need to hear, things like: acceptance, friendship, sympathy, and love.

Shaking hands when we first meet someone gives the message, "I accept you as a friend."

A kiss on the cheek or a hug means, "You are a close friend or a member of my family, someone I care for. You are important to me."

And when something dreadful happens, what we need most of all is someone to hold us tight.

When we read the stories of Jesus, we see how important touch was to him. Although he could heal someone without even being near them, again and again he chose to reach out a hand and touch the sick and the needy. He touched an untouchable leper; he put his fingers in a deaf man's ears; he held a dead girl by the hand and raised her to life.

You could expand this here by telling one of these stories. See **Mark 1:40–42; Mark 7:31–37; Mark 5:21–24, 35–43.**

Something to do

God made us in such a way that we all need touch — a kiss from Mum, a hug from a grandparent, a friend's hand on the shoulder. These things tell us that people love us. Jesus used touch to show God's love to those who needed it most.

We can share a bit of that love around: give someone a hug today!

7
God's glory on tour

Theme

Photos of comets can draw gasps of awe and wonder from children (and adults). Use them to share something of the splendours of God's creation.

NASA's Stardust mission is due to pass through the tail of comet Wild 2 in 2004 and bring back samples of interstellar dust in 2006. And on 4 July 2005, the Deep Impact mission plans to blast a hole in a comet and analyze the resulting debris. Media reports at these times could give special opportunities to use this talk.

You will need

- pictures of comets from books or from NASA's superb Astronomy Picture of the Day site. You can find these at *www.77talks.co.uk*.
- Alternatively, go to http://antwrp.gsfc.nasa.gov/apod/. At this site, click on Archive (near the bottom of the page) which brings up a list of past photos, organized by their dates. Suggested pictures are of comet Hale-Bopp at 1997 April 16, and a sungrazer comet at 2000 May 20. For more photos and information about comets, click on Search at the NASA site and enter "comets".

Presentation

Ideally, begin with the photo of comet Hale-Bopp. Some children will be old enough to remember having seen this comet in 1997. It was exceptionally bright and we will be lucky to see another comet as bright as this in our lifetimes.

A comet has been described as "a dirty snowball". It is

made of ice and dust. A comet itself is far too small to see — Hale-Bopp was just 40 kilometres (25 miles) across. But as it approaches the sun, it warms up and gives off gas and dust. That is the round "head" that we can see. Hale-Bopp's corona of dust and gas was some 100,000 kilometres (60,000 miles) wide.

This gas and dust is then blown straight out by the "solar wind" — hot plasma that streams out continuously from the sun's surface. That creates the tail of a comet. Hale-Bopp actually had two tails — a blue ionized gas tail and a white dust tail. The tails stretched millions of kilometres into space.

Comets orbit the sun in a strange way. Their orbit is a giant ellipse that takes them way out into deep space and then swinging back close to the sun. Hale-Bopp came closest to the sun on 1 April 1997 — 153 million kilometres (96 million miles) from the sun's north pole. (Earth is 150 million kilometres or 93 million miles from the sun.) Since then, it has begun a journey that will take it far away from the sun and the planets, not to return for another 4,000 years.

Spectacular sungrazers

Some comets come even closer to the sun. They are known as sungrazers. (Show the photo if you have it.) By using a disc to block out the sun, SOHO, the space-based SOlar and Heliospheric Observatory, has been able to take photos of these comets as they dive to within 50,000 kilometres (31,000 miles) of the sun. Not surprisingly, many sungrazers do not survive their encounter with the sun.

Comets have always fascinated people. The star of the Christmas story which led the wise men from the East to go in search of the baby king of the Jews may have been a comet.

Many centuries ago, David the shepherd boy spent some of his nights under the stars watching over the family's sheep. The first part of one of the songs he wrote goes like this:

Read **Psalm 19:1–4a**.

One writer translates the opening words as: **"God's glory is on tour in the skies."**[1] We don't know if David had a comet in his sight at the time, but that would be a pretty good description of one!

Something to think about

This song, Psalm 19, is a poet's response as he looks up at the sky, the sun, the moon and the stars. He is filled with wonder as he thinks that there is no place on earth where people can't just look up at any time of the day or night and see a reflection of God's power and splendour. People may have no Bible, no religious education, no scientific understanding, but something of the truth of the Creator is there for anyone with eyes to see.

Many of us who spend our days and nights under artificial light rarely turn our eyes to the skies. When a comet appears it encourages people to get away from their TV screens and gaze up at the wonders of the night sky. But we don't have to wait for a comet. Every clear night, the stars and planets are on show. Perhaps if we take time to gaze into the wonders of the night sky, our hearts will also respond to the revelation of **"God's glory . . . on tour in the skies"**.

NOTE

1 Eugene H. Peterson, *The Message* (Colorado Springs: Navpress, 1994). You might like to use Peterson's version for the whole of the reading.

8
10,000 trillion stars

Theme

More gasp-inducing photographs lead to humbling reflections on the power of the Creator and the reasons why he made the universe.

You will need

- The Hubble Space Telescope has given us amazing pictures of stars and galaxies. Some of these have been published in books or you can find them at the NASA Astronomy Picture of the Day site. For this talk you need at least Whirlpool Galaxy (2001 April 27) and the Milky Way (2000 January 30). These pictures have been copied to our own site: *www.77talks.co.uk* or you can find them at the NASA site, below.
- Another wonderful photo is "Moonlight, Mars, and Milky Way" taken by astrophotographer Barney Magrath in Hawaii. You can find this at http://antwrp.gsfc.nasa.gov/apod/. Click on Archive, then 2001 June 27. You could have this on display before you start.

Presentation

Show the photo of the Whirlpool Galaxy on the OHP. (If you can darken the room, so much the better.)

A galaxy is a kind of city of stars. It is a great swirl of dust, gas and stars slowly rotating in space. Astronomers believe that at the centre of most — maybe all — galaxies is a supergiant black hole.

The Whirlpool Galaxy is 30 million light-years away from earth. That means that it has taken the light from these stars 30 million years to reach us. The Whirlpool Galaxy is

60,000 light-years from side to side. It is one of the brightest and most beautiful galaxies in the sky, although you would need a telescope to see it.

Each of the stars in the galaxy is a sun like ours, some of them much bigger. Does anyone know how many stars there are in a galaxy like this? . . . 100 billion!

In **Psalm 147** in the Bible it says, God

> **determines the number of the stars and calls them each by name. Great is our Lord and mighty in power; his understanding has no limit.**
> *Psalm 147:4–5*, New International Version

A God who can create a galaxy of 100 billion stars is certainly "mighty in power"! But this isn't the only galaxy by a long way. We live in another galaxy. Does anyone know what our home galaxy is called? . . . The Milky Way.

Show picture.

100 billion neighbours

The Milky Way is a spiral galaxy that looks rather like the Whirlpool Galaxy. But because we are on one side of it we see it edge on. So this is a photo of our sun's 100 billion nearest neighbours!

That's just two galaxies. Would anyone like to guess how many galaxies there are in the whole universe? . . . 100 billion — the same number as there are stars in one galaxy.

So if there are 100 billion galaxies, each with 100 billion stars — that adds up to 10,000 trillion (10^{22}) stars in the universe!

The writer of that psalm says, **"He determines the number of stars."** If he determines the number of stars, why did he make 10,000 trillion of them? Surely that's going a bit over the top! After all, we only need one, our sun, to give us all the light and warmth we need on planet earth.

In recent years scientists have begun to tell us a different story. Apparently planet earth wouldn't be here at all if there weren't all those 10,000 trillion stars. The mass of the universe has to be exactly right. If the mass of the universe was either slightly larger or slightly smaller it would be impossible for earth — or any other planet like it — to exist. It seems that God wasn't going over the top in creating 100 billion galaxies. If you want to have one small planet that can support life — and human beings — you have to design a universe that big to start with. God knew what he was doing.

And he knew why he was doing it. Take a look at the person sitting next to you. If there weren't 10,000 trillion stars he or she would not be sitting there. And neither would you. You must be pretty important for God to go to all that trouble!

Surely the songwriter was right when he said, **"Great is our Lord and mighty in power; his understanding has no limit."**

9
Greater than
the force

Theme

Knowing the Creator personally. This is a talk to use when the latest in the *Star Wars* series is released, or it can be adapted to tie in with another sci-fi film or TV series.

You will need

• *Star Wars* videos or merchandising.

Presentation

Talk about the current *Star Wars* film. Many of us will be going to watch and enjoy it (including some ageing sci-fi fans who remember when the first ones came out!).

Great fun, but it is, of course, science fiction. The spaceships are models, the aliens are actors in costumes or digitally created, and lasers are just special effects.

The real universe we live in may not appear so exciting, but it is actually far more amazing than any science fiction. Take quasars, for example.

Quasars were discovered in 1964 and gave astronomers a real challenge. A quasar is no bigger than the solar system we live in, but it pours out more energy than hundreds of whole galaxies. We're talking about the heat and light of tens of thousands of billions of stars like our sun! It seems impossible.

But pictures from the Hubble Space Telescope have confirmed what is happening in a quasar. Imagine a huge, young galaxy with a supergiant black hole at its centre. This galaxy is colliding with another galaxy at more than 1 million kilometres per hour (60,000 m.p.h.), and the supergiant black hole is ripping gas and stars from the second galaxy. These stars are sucked into the black hole, and in their death throes they release incredible amounts of energy. Wow! The Death-Star has nothing on that!

Beyond our understanding

The Bible introduces us to the Creator of all this: God. Any Being who can design and create this incredible universe we live in must be infinitely too big for us to understand. And yet the Bible says we can know him — not just know some facts *about* him, but actually know *him* personally! Millions of Christians all over the world say that that is really true for them. They believe that in their spirit they can commune with the Spirit of God himself, the Creator of quasars and everything else. They call this communing with God, this being close to God, **"the fellowship of the Holy Spirit"**.

Something to think about

In the science fiction world of *Star Wars*, people say to each other, "May the force be with you." In the real world, Christians use these words:

> **May the grace of the Lord Jesus Christ, and the love of God, and the fellowship of the Holy Spirit, be with you.**
> *2 Corinthians 13:14*, New International Version

If you stop and think what that means, it's got to be a billion times more exciting than any make-believe "force"!

New Life Starts Here

**There's no technology that
can change the human heart**

10
Be refreshed

Theme

Inviting Jesus to clean us up and give us a new start brings life with a sparkle.

You will need

- a bottle of a well-known cola (preferably brought ice-cold in a cool-box) with two empty glasses; another glass of cola that has been left out a day or longer with one or two foreign bodies added, especially a dead fly or wasp; some cola-bottle sweets from the pocket-money counter; a bowl of water to wash a glass, and a cloth to dry it.

Presentation

Ask for a volunteer who fancies a glass of cola and pour them one, emphasizing how cool and refreshing it is. Ask for a second thirsty person and offer them the stale cola, complete with dead fly. Tell them how long it has been poured out and what it is likely to have in it. Will they drink it? . . . Will anyone? . . . It is good for nothing except to be thrown away.

Thank your volunteers. A big "Aaah!" for the second one who remains thirsty — and a cola-bottle sweet as a consolation!

Pour and hold up a second glass of fresh cola. This is how God intended life to be — full of sparkle, zest, joy. But the reality for a lot of people — especially many grown-ups — is that life has gone stale and flat. There may even be unpleasant things floating around in it that they would rather not talk about. Or perhaps they had big hopes and dreams, but what they have ended up with is — hold up another cola-bottle sweet — a big disappointment.

Jesus said,

I came to give life — life in all its fullness. *John 10:10*

"Life in all its fullness" — that could be a good advertising slogan for cola! It is certainly the real thing, not a cheap imitation or a stale left-over.

So if life is like this — the stale cola — how do we get it back to the way it was meant to be, like this — the sparkling cola? Let's see if we can find out from the beginning of Mark's story of Jesus.

Ducked in the river

Straight away in chapter 1 we find this rather strange man who wore designer clothes — well, he designed them himself from camel's hair! His name was John and his big thing was ducking people in the river. You might think he would get himself arrested for doing that — and he did later — but at this time loads of people were coming to see him. He told people that they needed to repent, which means to turn around and make a fresh start. Lots of people knew their lives were like stale cola with dead things floating around in it — the wrong things they had done and the mistakes they had made — so they were quite ready to repent and get rid of the mess of sin in their lives. [Empty the stale cola out of the glass.] Perhaps more people would do that today if they knew what was on offer.

Then John ducked them in the river. [Plunge the glass in the bowl, wash and dry it.] This was a sign that they were being cleaned up inside. It was called "baptizing", and the camel-hair shirt man got the nickname, John the Baptizer. Today we might call him John the Plunger or John the Ducker.

John the Baptizer also told people that someone far more important than him was coming, someone who would soak people not with water but with the Holy Spirit. And guess who came along? — Jesus.

Jesus asked John to baptize him — not that he needed to be cleaned up — and the Spirit of God came down on him in a way that was kind of visible. Some people said it looked like a dove.

A new sparkle

A few weeks later, John did get thrown in prison, but by then he had done his job. Now it was Jesus' turn to tell people some good news. Not only could they get cleaned up inside, but a whole new way of living was open to them — God's kingdom. [Pour a little fresh cola in the cleaned glass.] God's kingdom is where living is exciting and challenging, because God is in charge.

Then, to show this was not just words, Jesus started doing amazing things like healing people. Loads of people's lives got a new sparkle then. [Add some more cola to the glass.] You can find all this in just the first chapter of Mark's story of Jesus.

If you go on to read other parts of the story of Jesus, you will find that what John the Baptizer said about him came true. Jesus did soak people in the Holy Spirit, or fill them with the Spirit. Then their lives really started sparkling! [Fill the glass to the top.]

Ever since then, all down the centuries, people have been finding that it really works. I don't mean religion. Religion is just an unsatisfying substitute. I mean the real thing: **"life in all its fullness"**. Cheers! [Drink cola.]

www.77talks.co.uk

11
Finding treasure

Theme

The contrast between the remote possibility of winning the lottery and the certainty of the treasure of God's kingdom.

You will need

- a box containing a lottery ticket, a black marker pen, a treasure map (see *www.77talks.co.uk*), a blindfold, a crown (made out of card). Extra items if possible: a magnifying glass; a metal detector — or broom as a substitute (not in the box — hide it).

Presentation

Place the box on a table where it will be clearly visible. Show the objects one at a time and place them in view on the table. When all the objects are displayed, ask the children what they think the talk is going to be about . . . It is going to be about treasure.

One way lots of people think they can get treasure is by playing the national lottery. I wonder how likely they are to win the jackpot? Let's see if we can find out. We're going to give one person the same chance of finding something as of winning the first prize in the lottery.

Ask for a volunteer who doesn't mind being blindfolded — *Henry*. Now you need ten more volunteers who all have fair hair, if possible. Line them up at the front.

What we are going to do is choose one of these people and then choose one hair on their head. Then we'll mark that hair with a marker pen. But first we'll blindfold *Henry*.

Choose one of the ten, separate out a single hair, hold it against a piece of white card or paper, and mark the end few centimetres with the marker pen.

Do you know how many hairs you have on your head? Blond-haired people have around 145,000 hairs, dark-haired people around 120,000, and red-heads 90,000.

One hair on ten heads

Now here's the test for *Henry*. He has to see if he can find the hair with the black mark on it among these ten people. Ask *Henry* to choose a number between one and ten, place him behind the chosen person in the line, and get him to single out one hair. He might need a bit of help. Then take off his blindfold and hand him a magnifying glass, holding a piece of paper behind the chosen hair. Is it the right one?!

What chance did *Henry* have of finding the right hair? There are ten people here, each with around 145,000 hairs. How many hairs is that? . . . 1,450,000. *Henry* had one chance in nearly 1.5 million of finding the right hair. I said this was going to be like the chance of winning the first prize on the lottery! To do that properly we would have needed **100** people in the line, not ten. Getting the right six numbers to win the lottery is the same as finding the one right hair from the heads of 100 people.

Thank the volunteers and ask them to sit down.

Playing the lottery looks like just about the worst possible way you could choose of finding treasure. Let's see what we've got here that might be more helpful. This treasure map, for example. It has some words written round the outside. Get a child to read it:

The kingdom of heaven is like treasure hidden in a field. One day a man found the treasure. The man was

**very happy to find the treasure. He went and sold
everything he owned to buy that field.** *Matthew 13:44*

Jesus was telling a story about someone finding treasure. If
it was today, they would probably use a metal detector.
(This is the place for a bit of action with your broom/
metal detector.)

Imagine the excitement of discovering a whole chest full
of gold and silver coins! The trouble was, the field didn't
belong to the man in the story. What could he do? He
hadn't got enough money to buy the field. There was only
one thing for it — bury the treasure again and sell
everything he had to raise enough money. Car, TV, clothes,
even his metal detector — everything had to go to raise
the money to buy the field.

A guaranteed winner

Buying the field cost a lot more than buying a lottery
ticket. But see the difference. When a person buys a lottery
ticket they only have one chance in 14 million of winning
the big prize — the same as finding the right hair on 100
people's heads. But when this man bought the field he
knew he'd won the jackpot. He already knew the treasure
was there. He was a guaranteed winner!

But hold on. What is the treasure Jesus is talking about? Is
it a chest of gold coins, or something else? There's a clue
on the map. Lets read it again: **"The kingdom of heaven
is like treasure hidden in a field."** The kingdom of
heaven — I wonder what that is? Is there a clue in the
things that came out of the box? What haven't we used
yet? . . . The crown. A kingdom needs a king, and a king
wears a crown. Who do you think is the king of the
kingdom of heaven? . . . Jesus, or God. The kingdom of
heaven is God's kingdom. It's where everything happens
the way he wants it to happen.

Just think about what it would be like in a place where Jesus was king. Do you think there would be people hurting each other or fighting? . . . Do you think there would be some people starving because other people were greedy and selfish? . . . Do you think things would be spoiled by waste and pollution? . . . Do you think people would be bored or miserable? . . . Do you think there would be anyone there who didn't have exciting things to do? . . . No.

People hope to win the lottery because they think they will be able to buy lots of things to make them happy. But in God's kingdom of heaven people have already got all they need to make them happy. Just being there is the treasure. The man in the story was bursting with happiness and excitement when he found it.

[Hold up the crown and the lottery ticket for everyone to see.]

I wonder which you think is the best way of finding treasure?

A prayer

Father God, please help me not to waste my time looking for the wrong kind of treasure or looking for treasure in the wrong place. Please show me what is the real treasure in this life, and how I can find it. Amen.

12
The fear of death

Theme

How to have a life that cannot be destroyed.

You will need

- a glass of water.
- a sari or some sari material if possible.

Presentation

Drink the glass of water.

If I'd drunk that water in Britain in the 19th century — or if I drank it in Bangladesh now — I might be dead in 24 hours. I might die because the water could be contaminated with one of the world's deadliest diseases — cholera. Just imagine living with the fear that your next drink could kill you or a member of your family!

The cholera bacteria cause severe diarrhoea and vomiting within four to twelve hours, which leads to severe dehydration (loss of fluid in the body). More than half the people who catch cholera and are not treated die, sometimes within 18 hours of the first symptoms. Antibiotics are no use in treating cholera, and vaccination is not very much help.

How have we managed to get rid of the fear of cholera in the Western world almost completely? By a huge investment in sewerage systems in the 19th century. This kept polluted water — the water and waste from toilets — separate from fresh water.

No money for sewers

Many parts of the world do not have such sewerage systems, or the money to build them. Even the wood to boil water to kill the bacteria is too scarce in Bangladesh.

But scientists have found a remarkably simple way to filter the cholera bacteria out of water. It is the sari — and every woman in Bangladesh has one.

The breakthrough came when a team of scientists discovered that the cholera bacteria live inside the guts of tiny organisms in the water. Although the bacteria themselves are too small to be filtered out, the carrier organisms are trapped very efficiently in four layers of sari material, and 99% are removed. Simply hanging the sari out to dry in the sun is enough to kill the trapped bacteria and sterilize the cloth — for free!

If this proves to work long-term in everyday life, many lives will be spared and many people saved from a potent fear of death.

Something to think about

Because of the efforts of our great-great-grandparents in building sewerage systems, we can drink water without fear of death. But we can never get rid of the fear of death altogether. After all, we are all going to die one day! Christians believe this is why Jesus came. It says in the Bible that people were like slaves all their lives because of the fear of death (Hebrews 2:15). The message of Easter is that death need no longer be feared. Paul wrote:

> **Our Saviour Christ Jesus . . . destroyed death, and through the Good News he showed us the way to have life that cannot be destroyed.** *2 Timothy 1:10*

For many families in Bangladesh it must be worth finding out how to use their everyday clothing to protect themselves from cholera. Christians believe it is worth anybody's time to find out about **"the way to have life that cannot be destroyed"**.

13
I tell you the truth

Theme

Jesus is the truth-teller, and his truth leads to the prize of eternal life.

You will need

- a list of true or false statements (there is one provided on the *www.77talks.co.uk* website); possibly a large dice.
- three or four boxes, one containing enough sweets as prizes for one team.

Presentation

Divide the children into two or three teams and run a "true or false" quiz. Scoring can be with a giant dice to add an element of chance and bigger scores.

When the quiz is finished, show the boxes. The prize for the winning team is in one of them. You will tell them which one. The problem is, you may not be telling the truth, so they will have to decide between themselves whether to believe you and take the box you have indicated or to choose another one! Whether to believe you or not leads to some interesting — and possibly heated! — discussions.

If the winning team chooses wrongly, then the second-placed team have a chance, again with you telling them which one it is. (With three teams you could have four boxes, so that there is always a chance for any team — or none — to get the prize.)

Hoax death threats

Not knowing whether someone is telling the truth or not is very frustrating. It can lead to doubts, arguments, indecision, bad choices. Imagine the problem faced by the police when they get a phone call saying there is a bomb in a public place. If it is a hoax and they clear the street or railway station or whatever, then there is terrific disruption for nothing. If the call is genuine but they choose not to believe it, lives may be lost. No wonder the police and the courts come down very hard on people who make hoax bomb threats.

No less than 78 times in the gospel records Jesus says, "I tell you the truth . . ." Sometimes Jesus is talking about life and death situations. For example, in John 5:24 Jesus says,

> **I tell you the truth. Whoever hears what I say and believes in the One who sent me has eternal life. He will not be judged guilty. He has already left death and has entered into life.**

Was Jesus a hoaxer, a liar who led people up the garden path? It is an important question because, as Jesus himself made plain, it is a life and death question. If he was a liar, then he was one of the worst men who has ever lived, because hundreds of millions of people have been taken in by him for more than 20 centuries.

But the things that he did, and the way he lived and taught others to live — do these seem like the life and teaching of a liar and a cheat? Even many who don't call themselves Christians would never call him a bad man; they respect him as a great man and teacher.

The most brilliant mind

But if Jesus was not a liar, then the things he said were the most important things anyone has ever said in the history of the world. He is the man with the most brilliant mind, the man with the greatest understanding, the most gifted teacher, and the most caring and compassionate person who has ever lived. He is the only man who has ever truly known the mysteries of life and death.

To hold a Bible, and to read as Jesus says, **"I tell you the truth,"** or even simply, **"I tell you,"** is to hold in your hands everything you need to know about this life or the life to come.

When Jesus says, **"I tell you the truth,"** you know you are going to find the prize. And the prize is eternal life.

14
Bags of goods

Theme

What we are on the inside can match how we appear on the outside if we let Jesus remake us.

You will need

- a selection of shopping bags from stores in your area. (If you explain what you want them for, shops will be pleased to let you have one.)
- items to go inside the bags, some appropriate, some not.
- a dustbin liner with a hole cut in the bottom for a child's head to go through.

Presentation

Get some volunteers to guess what is inside your different shopping bags. Some can be appropriate items, some decidely not — like a pair of smelly socks in a bag from an expensive store. You may even find one or two punning examples, such as a jar of balti paste in a Curry's bag.

You could have one or more bags where the child who correctly guesses the contents gets to keep it.

Unless we are really snobbish and carry around a bag from an expensive store just to be seen with it, what really matters is the contents of the bag, not what it says on the outside. God is looking for people who don't just look good on the outside, but who are right on the inside.

Jesus had a word for people who looked better than they really were — hypocrites. One time, he even said such people were like tombs in a graveyard — painted to look nice on the outside, but full of bones and rotting things inside. That's a lot worse than a posh bag with smelly socks inside. Jesus could be pretty rude about hypocrites!

There is another kind of bagful that Jesus does not want any of us to be.

[Get a volunteer and put the dustbin liner over them, so that their head pokes through the hole.]

Jesus does not think that any of us is like this, a bag full of rubbish to be thrown away. He made us. He loves us. We are precious to him. St Paul says, **"You were bought at a price."** (1 Corinthians 6:20) That price was the death of Jesus on the cross. Nobody ever paid a price greater than that.

Whatever rubbish there is inside us, Jesus doesn't want us to pretend it isn't there, like the hypocrites do. He wants us to invite him into our lives, to clean us up, to make us the wonderful person he designed us to be.

Proud of our purchases

We go to the shops and buy something, perhaps something we have been wanting for a long time. We take it home and get it out of the bag. We are pleased. We are proud. We want to show it off to our friends. Jesus wants something like that, too. He paid the price for us. He wants one day to take us home to the place he has prepared for us. What we are on the outside won't be needed any more. It can be thrown away, like a plastic shopping bag. The real us, the person we are on the inside, will then be clearly seen.

No one would want to be a hypocrite on that day, to be seen to be just old, rotting bones, to be seen to have wasted his or her life. But those who have invited Jesus into their lives will be seen to be perfect, wonderful, precious, of everlasting worth. That's the way Jesus will have made them.

Something to do

If the situation is appropriate, listeners may be given the
opportunity to invite Jesus into their lives. Or it could be
suggested that they explore this further themselves by
visiting the Narrow Gate pages of the *www.jubilee-kids.org*
website.

15
Light from behind bars

Theme

The remarkable true story of David Lant, a criminal serving a life sentence for murdering another prisoner, and how his life has been radically changed. He cannot ever undo the damage he has done, but today he spends his time helping others, producing Braille to enable blind people to read.

You will need

- a sample of Braille, if possible. (Try your local library.)
- the codebreaker and translation of Luke 4:18 on page 72 or from the *www.77talks.co.uk* website. This could be photocopied and used as a follow-up, or printed onto acetate to show on the OHP.

Presentation

David Lant was once one of the most dangerous men in British prisons. He made his first appearance in the juvenile court when he was eight years old. Then he spent 20 years locked up in approved schools and special hospitals. Finally, he was sentenced to life imprisonment for murdering another patient at Broadmoor Hospital. So what made an ordinary boy turn into a violent criminal?

David had an older brother, John. But one day David learned from a stranger that John was not his brother at all. And his mum was not his real mother. He was adopted, and his adopted family had decided not to tell him. (That was quite normal in those days.)

Even now, he still remembers how painful this discovery

was: "I had loved, adored, idolized John. Now I felt that he had betrayed me — and in the worst possible way — to a stranger. From that moment my world crumbled around me. My love for John turned instantly to deep hatred towards him and towards everyone in general." The only outlet for this hatred that David could find was violence. He turned to crime.

He was sent to a special kind of school for young people who had committed crimes, and later to prison. Every time he was released, he would slip back into bad ways: "Nothing seemed to stop me. I just continued running away and committing more crimes." And so it went on, until eventually David found himself sentenced to life imprisonment for taking part in the murder of another prisoner.

After he was given the life sentence, he concentrated on learning how to beat the prison system: "Whenever I thought that I had been unjustly treated, I noted it down in what I called my 'box of hatred'. I would have died rather than let that 'box of hatred' out of my sight."

Letters

After many years in prison, David was filmed for a television documentary called *Lifer*. Some people who saw the programme started writing to him. One of them was a Christian woman called Margaret. She told him she was praying for him. David didn't believe in God, and took no notice of what she said in her letter.

However, he did notice a change in Peter, one of the lads on his wing. It turned out that Peter had become a Christian. He said he was also praying that David would meet Jesus. At that time, David was still not interested in God: "Not in a thousand years will I become a Christian!" There was no way you would catch *him* going all "religious" like that.

Soon after this, David was in his cell one night when he suddenly realized that he did not like the person that he had become. He didn't want to go on hurting and hating others. He wanted to change, like Peter had done, but he knew he needed help, special help. So David found himself kneeling on the floor, apologizing to God for everything he had done and asking God to help him to change into a better person.

The vilest offender

A couple of weeks later, David woke up in the middle of the night and started whistling a tune. It stayed with him all through the next morning. At dinner-time Peter asked him, "Do you know the words to that tune?" David said he didn't; Peter got out a hymn book and began to read these words:

> **The vilest offender who truly believes,**
> **That moment from Jesus a pardon receives.**

David said: "I knew that Jesus had spoken to me. I was that 'vilest offender'. I had received a pardon for every one of my horrendous sins because I truly believed in him."

Today, David is a very different person. He is still in prison, and like the rest of us he still gets it wrong sometimes, but it is hard to believe such a caring person could ever have got his kicks out of hurting others. Instead, he has committed his life to helping people in difficulty. He translates books from English (and other languages) into Braille, so that blind and visually impaired people are able to read them. He has even won an award for his services to people suffering from blindness throughout the world.

He is also happily married to a woman called Christine whom he met through his work, and is looking forward to the time when he finishes his sentence and they can be together. He is living proof of the fact that no matter how bad our lives may be, we all have the chance to begin again.

Something to do

Give out copies of the Braille text — or show it on the OHP — and see if the children can translate it into something Jesus said.

NOTES

Condensed from David Lant's own testimony, *Adopted!*

David's Braille ministry operates under LIGHTWING PROJECTS, Registered Charity no. 1016529. For further details visit the website at http://www.wyrecompute.oaktree.co.uk/lightwing.

BRAILLE ALPHABET

1	2	3	4	5	6	7	8	9	0
a	b	c	d	e	f	g	h	i	j	k	l	m	n	o	p	q	r	s

| t | u | v | w | x | y | z | | . | : | ; | ? | ! | * |

| opening quotation | closing quotation | numeral sign |

Can you decipher this?

(Luke 4:18)

www.77talks.co.uk

I saw a star fall

Theme

Comets or meteors may wipe out human life on the earth, but the big decision remains the same: Whose side are you on?

You will need

- a picture of an asteroid, printed onto an OHP transparency if possible. You will find some pictures at *www.77talks.co.uk* and a link to the NASA Astronomy Picture of the Day website.
- a Bible: Revelation 8:6–9:2.

Presentation

Show a picture of an asteroid, or ask who has seen a shooting star.

Pieces of rock from space hit the earth every day. As they enter the atmosphere they burn up, creating the brief flash of a shooting star. Some are large enough for bits to land on earth. About once every 1,000 years a rock nearly 100 metres (300 feet) in diameter strikes our planet, big enough to cause a tidal wave if it lands in the sea.

But what would happen if a really large meteor was on collision course with the earth?

Actually, it is not a matter of *if* but *when*. The last time it happened was maybe less than 4,400 years ago, around 2350 BC, a mere eye-blink in cosmic time. At that time there seems to have been a great environmental catastrophe, and civilizations collapsed. Mud-brick buildings in northern Syria appear to have been destroyed by what is described as a "blast from the sky".

The K-T event

So could it happen again? The bad news is, yes, it could. The good news is that a collision with a massive asteroid, over 1km across, is more rare, happening only once in millions of years. But an asteroid that size would create a global catastrophe, wiping out many species of plants and animals.

Is that what killed the dinosaurs? Around 65 million years ago they disappeared, together with about 70% of all species then living on earth. This is known as the K-T event (the Cretaceous-Tertiary Mass Extinction event). Could it have been caused by an asteroid or comet hitting the earth? In 1990 came evidence that it was. A 65 million-year-old crater, 180 kilometres (112 miles) wide, was discovered under layers of sediment in the Yucatan Peninsula region of Mexico. It would have taken an asteroid ten kilometres (6.5 miles) wide to make this crater — big enough to cause massive global disruption.

The last book in the Bible, the book of Revelation, describes some great environmental catastrophes, including what sounds like a description of the earth being struck, perhaps by a chain of comet pieces like those that spectacularly hit Jupiter in 1994.

Read **Revelation 8:6 – 9:2**.

It's a pretty terrifying picture. Christians have different ideas about what it means. Some think it is a prediction of what will actually happen in the future. Some think it is using coded picture language to describe the persecution suffered by Christians in the Roman empire.

Great war

But everyone agrees in general what the book of Revelation is about: there is a great war going on between the powers of good and evil. In the end, God will deal once and for all with evil. But each person must decide for themselves which side they are on. Many people would prefer not to think about that decision. They bury themselves in their work, or fill their lives with TV and music and entertainment so that they don't have to think. But just doing nothing allows the evil around us to grow.

For each one of us personally, it makes no difference whether we are hit by a twelve-mile-wide asteroid or a number 11 bus! One thing is for sure: we will each meet our own personal end sometime within the next 100 years (a lot sooner for some of us!).

If a big asteroid is headed in our direction, we won't be able to duck it. We can't duck the big question either: **Whose side are you on?**

NOTE

This could be expanded — or followed up — by asking the question, **Who will save us?** In Hollywood blockbusters the current megastar gets to nuke the offending asteroid and save the earth. In the real-life war between good and evil . . . well, most readers of this book know the answer to that one!

www.77talks.co.uk

17
Only the scars
tell the story

Theme

Young Frenchman Franck Fama survived a serious motor cycle accident and experienced a recovery his surgeon described as "miraculous". Here is his story to tell or to use as an illustration.

You will need

- A photo of Franck can be found at *www.77talks.co.uk* if you wish to use it.

Presentation

It was a hot June night in 1989 when three friends came out of a disco in the Ardeche region in southern France. 22-year-old Franck swung his 600cc Suzuki onto a dirt track and joined his friends in racing to a point where they could join the road.

On the road, Franck found himself alone. The other two had shot ahead. He leaned left into a bend, hugging the middle of the road. Suddenly he saw the car. It was taking the bend wide, straddling the white line. All he remembers of the next moment is the loud crack as his left arm hit the front of the car.

Thirteen months in hospital

Lying beside the road, he regained consciousness to find one of his friends kneeling over him, crying. *Am I dying?* he thought. *Am I cut in two? Is that why he's crying?* Then, *I want to sleep. I want to sleep.* And he lost consciousness again.

At the hospital, doctors worked to piece together his broken bones. His right leg was almost severed. A long metal pin holding the bone together from a previous motor bike accident just six months before probably saved it from amputation. There were four breaks in his left leg, and his left arm was very badly smashed. It was the beginning of a thirteen-month stay in hospital.

Coming that close to death makes anyone think about the meaning of life. As a young teenager, Franck had decided he wanted to be free of the things he had learned in his local Catholic church as a child. But the way his life was going now didn't seem to be of much use to him; he decided to give it all to God. He even wrote his decision down on a piece of paper. He felt peaceful, although nothing much more seemed to change at the time.

Nerve grafts

Six months after the accident, his left arm was paralyzed. He could expect to regain a little movement, but some of the nerves had been completely cut. The surgeon decided to try a kind of operation that was new in France. It involved taking sections of nerves from his legs. These were several centimetres long but not much thicker than a piece of thread.

Then they cut through the muscles at the top of his chest to graft the nerve sections into his left shoulder and arm. After that it was a matter of patience. Would the nerves grow and join up again? Would the muscles in his arm start responding to messages from his brain once more?

During the long months in hospital Franck bought a Bible and started to read it right through. Reading the stories of Jesus and his disciples, he thought, *That's the truth; that's the right way to live. But why don't we see that now? Why aren't there any Christians like that today?*

77

As he read the Bible, two things started happening. He began to look at life much more positively. And he began to get movement back into his left arm. It progressed so quickly that his surgeon could hardly believe it. "A miracle," was his verdict. The physiotherapist, too, thought it was unbelievable.

Of seven young men on the ward with paralyzed arms, Franck was the only one to recover. He even took to keeping it still in front of the others, in order not to upset them!

He was allowed out of hospital for a few weeks, but then it was back in for a further six months. This time the doctors were going to break both his legs again and reset the bones straighter.

Every morning, he was wheeled down to spend half an hour with a blind physiotherapist who was working with him on his left arm. The physio was a Christian. They spent the time talking about the Bible, and each day, the physio gave Franck a couple of Bible verses he had learned by heart.

It's all too simple!

What Franck found difficult to understand was how the Bible stories seemed to be so real and so relevant to the physio. It all seemed too simple!

When the time came for him to leave hospital, the physio invited him to an adult baptism in a large church in Lyon. They arrived late to find some 400 people praising God. It was very lively, and different from anything Franck had known of church before. "This is strange," he said to himself, "but there is something in this praise that is really powerful."

He started going to another branch of the same church and realized he had found what he had read about in the

Bible — a faith that people really lived out in their everyday lives. There *were* Christians today like those he had read about after all! He felt he had found what he had been looking for all those years. He was baptized himself on 18 April 1993.

Unexpected bonuses

Seeing Franck today climbing mountains or jumping off ten metre cliffs into the Ardeche river, you would never know how close he came to losing a leg or the use of an arm. Only the scars tell the story.

And there are two other unexpected bonuses. Before the accident he was a jeweller, but he really wanted to do something to help other people. Now he works as a nurse. He sees that as a real blessing.

And the second bonus? Three months after he was baptized, he went to a Christian conference. There he met an English girl — and it was love at first sight! Franck and Rebecca were married four years later and baby Esther was born to them in 2001.

18
Just a crowd of silly sheep?

Theme

Jesus lays down his life for his followers and opens the way to eternal life.

You will need

- You could use the cartoon *Silly sheep* on the *www.77talks.co.uk* website.

Presentation

Who has been for a walk in the country and knows what a cattle grid is?

A cattle grid is a series of bars set over a hole in the road. Cars can cross it easily, and people with care, but animals are put off because their feet might slip through and they could injure themselves. Cattle grids are often used on roads in the country and at farm entrances because it saves people having to stop and get out of their cars twice in order to open and close a gate.

But cunning sheep in a village in the New Forest in southern England have learned a new trick for getting to the lush grass on the other side — or to the flowers in people's gardens.

They seem to choose one of their number to lie down on the grid, while the others scramble across her body. [Show the picture.]

Commando technique

It's the same kind of technique as that which commandos use for getting across barbed wire. The commandos select one unfortunate to lie on his rifle across the barbed wire, and the others walk across him. Ouch!

In one village, people had to install extra protection for their gardens — electric fences in some cases. The church had to put up barriers to stop the sheep eating the flowers off the graves.

Who said sheep were silly? Perhaps this is what you get when you leave sheep to their own devices instead of having a full-time shepherd to watch over them, as in the old days.

Jesus once talked about himself being like a shepherd. In those days there were no cattle grids, but there was a far greater danger — wolves.

This is what Jesus said:

> **I am the good shepherd. The good shepherd gives his life for the sheep. The worker who is paid to keep the sheep is different from the shepherd who owns them. So when the worker sees a wolf coming, he runs away and leaves the sheep alone. Then the wolf attacks the sheep and scatters them. The man runs away because he is only a paid worker. He does not really care for the sheep. I am the good shepherd. I know my sheep as my Father knows me . . . I give my life for the sheep.** *John 10:11–15*

Another translation puts that last line, "**I lay down my life for the sheep.**"

A New Forest sheep may lay down her body for others to walk across, but we can't imagine her laying down her life for her friends. The Bible teaches that Jesus did just that on Good Friday. He allowed himself to be taken prisoner, to be tried and crucified. He chose to lay down his life.

By laying down his life like this, Jesus provided a way over for his "sheep" (his followers) — a way into heaven. The sheep get across the cattle grid to the fresh green grass they know they like. People sometimes think of heaven like that: more of the life they know on earth, only nicer. But the Bible teaches that heaven is unimaginably wonderful, beyond the bounds of space and time, beyond the power of human words to describe.

Something to do

We don't know if one sheep can feel grateful to another for lying down and letting her walk over her. Certainly, commandos must feel grateful when one of their friends lies down on the barbed wire to let them cross unharmed. It's not surprising that Christians want to meet regularly and sing songs of praise because Jesus was prepared to lay down his life for them.

Sing a suitable praise song known to the group.

19
Robots don't win prizes

Theme

God gave us freedom, and if we freely choose to be guided by him we will win the greatest prize of all.

You will need

- an assistant dressed as a robot (the simplest costume to use is an all-in-one protective garment as sold in car-accessory shops) with a duster, brush, etc; a TV remote control.
- a suitable prize hidden well out of sight in the hall you are using.

Presentation

Inform the group that you are tired of housework and have acquired some cutting-edge home-help technology — a robot. Press a button on the TV remote and your assistant enters.

Give a series of instructions so that the robot goes round cleaning up — including dusting some of the audience. Extol the virtues of this robot that never gets tired, never breaks anything while washing up, never complains.Try the robot on double speed for an extra fast clean-up job. Eventually its batteries start to run down and you have to send it off — very slowly and jerkily — for a recharge. (Or it could even break down altogether and have to be carried off by two previously primed volunteers.)

God could have made robots if he had wanted to. In fact, he has made all kinds of things, from atoms to galaxies, that run as he programmed them to. (God's programmes are what we call the laws of physics.)

But imagine living alone with a robot and never seeing another living person, never having a friend to talk to or share things with. What a deadly existence! There is something so different, so wonderful, about a living person.

The very reason God created the universe was so that we could exist, living beings, each one of us different. He made people. But when he made us, he took the risk of making us free — unlike robots — free to go and do whatever we want to do and be whatever we want to be.

Happy to choose

Now I would like a volunteer who is not like a robot, someone who is happy to choose to do what I am going to ask. It could be doing some cleaning up — or it could be something nicer.

When you have a volunteer, explain that you are going to ask them to find something hidden in the room. In the time-honoured fashion, you help them by saying, "cold" — "warm" — "hot" etc. Guide them to find the prize, which they show to the others and keep.

There is all the difference in the world between a robot which only follows instructions and a person who freely chooses to be guided by God. You would never think of giving your video recorder a prize or treating your washing machine. They are just robots who follow your instructions blindly. But God rewards those who listen to his voice and follow his guidance in their lives.

The prophet Isaiah knew this. He talked about people who live as God wants them to live, people who are just and generous. Then he said,

The Lord will guide you always; he will satisfy your needs in a sun-scorched land and will strengthen your frame.   *Isaiah 58:11*

We may not live in a sun-scorched land — although we might wish we did sometimes! — but the promise is good for wherever we live: God will guide us, care for us and meet our needs, even in difficult circumstances. And his reward goes far beyond that. It includes all the wonderful things that Jesus said he is going to prepare for us in his Father's house.

And why? Because we are not robots. Because we are free living beings, able to respond to God's love and choose to follow his guiding voice. Robots don't win prizes, but God rewards those who choose to love and listen to him.

20
Some adults
never live

Theme

Sooner or later we all face the challenge of playing it safe or answering the call of Jesus and being a risk-taker.

You will need

- Nothing needed.

Presentation

A girl was in hospital. She had leukemia. One of the hospital chaplains came to visit her. **"I'm going to die,"** said the girl. **"But I don't mind. Because I've really lived. Some adults never live. Why don't they?"**

"Some adults never live." You might ask the children if they think this is true and, if so, why? (Be prepared for some interesting and challenging answers!)

Is it because some adults are scared of taking risks, always wanting to play it safe? A radiotherapist who treats cancer patients said that some people only really start living when they get cancer. Perhaps that is because they know they cannot play safe any longer; they've got nothing to lose — they are going to die anyway.

What kind of adult do you think you are going to be?

Let's try the fishing test. Imagine you are a few years older, say, just turned 20. Although you are still young, you've got a small business with a couple of people working for you. You are never going to be rich or famous, but you can be pretty sure of living comfortably for the rest of your life.

But you also reckon that the world could be a better place than it is now, and you are looking for some answers to what life is all about. One day, you meet a man who is like nobody you've ever met before. And he does seem to have some answers — lots of answers. You start to spend some time with him. Wherever he goes, amazing things happen, things that nobody can explain. He really seems to change people's lives for the better. Everyone is talking about him.

Then one day, he comes along when you're working and says, **"Drop what you are doing and come and work with me. There's no money in it, but you are going to change people's lives."**

What do you do? Play it safe and stick with your job? Or take a risk, not knowing where it might lead you?

You might like to see if a couple of the children will tell you what they would do, and why.

Not foolish risk-takers

We said that this was the "fishing test". That is because, when something like this actually happened, there were three young men and their business was fishing. Their names were Peter, James and John. The man who challenged them to leave their fishing business and go with him was Jesus. They accepted the challenge.

Peter, James and John were risk-takers. But they weren't foolish risk-takers. For a start, these young men had their holy book — what we now call the Old Testament of the Bible. They knew that God had promised to send a Saviour, a Messiah. Because they knew something of what God was like, they had an idea of what the Messiah would be like. So they were not going to be easily taken in. Then they spent enough time with Jesus and saw enough of what he did, to know that he was an extraordinary man with extraordinary power. They also saw that he had the kind of goodness they would expect of someone truly sent by God. So they took the risk.

Did they regret it? Absolutely not. Years later, Peter wrote:

> **Through his glory and goodness, [Jesus] gave us the very great and rich gifts he promised us. With those gifts you can share in being like God.** *2 Peter 1:4*

And John wrote:

> **He who gives life was shown to us. We saw him, and we can give proof about it . . . We write this to you so that you can be full of joy with us.** *1 John 1:2a, 4*

Clearly, these men thought that leaving their fishing business to go with Jesus was the best decision they ever took. It may have started out as a risk, but they ended up with proof that Jesus was the one they believed him to be, the Son of God.

"Some adults never live. Why don't they?" Peter, James and John lived life to the full. Both James and Peter were eventually executed, but they had discovered that a life following Jesus was worth any risk. They knew by heart something that Jesus had often said:

> **Whoever wants to save his life will lose it. And whoever gives his life for me will save it.** *Luke 9:24*

"Some adults never live." Perhaps they are so scared that they might lose their security or their reputation or their pension that they miss out on the real meaning and adventure of life. In trying to make themselves safe and secure they actually run the biggest risk of all: **"Whoever wants to save his life will lose it,"** said Jesus.

Sooner or later, everyone faces a version of the fishing test that is designed just for them. You can tell how a lot of adults have answered their test by what is important to them. Maybe they'll get another chance. Maybe they won't. What about you? What will you do when your "fishing test" comes?

Live Today Supernaturally

With God's life within us,
the possibilities are endless

21
The 160km crawl

Theme

With God's power working in us, he can achieve in us far more than we can imagine.

You will need

- a piece of string or ribbon six metres long and a ballooon.
- a road atlas, to find a place approximately 160 kilometres (100 miles) from your town.

Presentation

Ask a child to crawl out to the front. Can they remember crawling as a baby? Can they guess how far they crawled before they were two years old? . . . The average baby crawls 160 kilometres (100 miles) by the age of two. That's as far as from here to [insert appropriate place-name]. How ever did our knees survive!

Ask for another volunteer who has a reputation as a chatterbox. Can they tell you a new word they have learned in the past day? . . . How many new words do the children think they learn each day? . . . After the age of two, we all learn a new word on average every two hours for the next ten years. That's getting on for 4,500 new words every year, mostly without ever realizing that we are learning them. No wonder some people never seem to stop talking!

Get another child to blow up a balloon. If all the air they breathed out filled balloons, how many would they fill by the time they got to 22 years old? . . . 3.5 million. That's almost as much hot air as politicians produce in an average week!

50 years' hair growth

Get another child with long hair to tell you how long it has taken her to grow her hair that long. If she didn't cut it for 50 years, how long would it be? . . . Ask the child to hold one end of the piece of string on her head and stretch out the rest down the hall — six metres (20 feet). She would need a couple of full-time bridesmaids to follow her around carrying it!

Actually, hair usually stops growing and drops out by the time it gets to 90 centimetres (three feet) long. (So, did *John* have a 90cm ponytail where his bald spot is now?)

Did you know that was what your mind and body were capable of? And lots more beside, of course. Unless you are an extremely big-headed person, you can do far more than you think you can.

If you can grow twelve centimetres (five inches) of hair a year, or learn twelve new words a day without thinking about it, how much can the all-powerful God do in you and through you?

Here is what Paul said in one of his letters:

> **With God's power working in us, God can do much, much more that anything we can ask or think of. To him be glory in the church and in Christ Jesus for all time, for ever and ever. Amen.** *Ephesians 3:20–21*

No doubt Paul never dreamed that the letters he was writing would be read in churches and homes all over the world 2,000 years later and would transform the lives of millions of people.

At this point, you might want to refer to a story you have told recently about someone God used to bring about real change in the lives of others.

Something to think about

When God's power works in us, it isn't something for us to be proud of, any more than we should be proud because we crawled 160km (100 miles) before we were two. The glory goes to God — in the church and in Jesus. But we can be pleased. And we can ask God to fill us with his love so that his power can work through us and make the world a better place.

22
In-body navigation aid

Theme

The Bible and the Holy Spirit together provide the ultimate aid to travelling life's journey.

You will need

- a road atlas.
- If you are doing this in church, you could have some simple plans of the church and two or three sets of instructions for getting from the church door to different significant points in the church.

Presentation

Talk about an incident when you or someone known to you got lost and could have done with a map (or the ability to read the one they had!).

If using the church plans, this is an opportunity to get some of the children moving around — and learning the names of different parts of the church as they do it.

These days it is helpful to have more than just a road atlas when you are travelling in a car. You may know exactly where you are going, but a traffic jam on a motorway can delay you far more than getting lost. For information on the road conditions ahead and how to avoid trouble spots, an in-car navigation system is very helpful.

Ask if anyone or their parents has one and can tell you about it.

We often talk about life being a journey. The Bible is a brilliant aid to travelling this journey. It not only maps out where we have come from, but where we are going to. It gives loads of advice on how to travel, things to avoid on the way, and good companions to share the journey with. It is also full of travellers' tales — the stories of other people's journeys, the times they stupidly took a wrong turning and got lost, how they got back on the right road, and lots more. Reading these travellers' tales — the stories of Abraham, David, Paul and many, many more — really helps us get the most out of our own journey.

Instant messaging service

But as you read these stories, you discover something else. Although these travellers lived centuries ago, they all had a kind of in-car navigation. (Except in those days it was probably in-camel navigation!) They had an instant messaging service. Sometimes it warned them of trouble ahead; sometimes it gave them advice on the best road to take; sometimes it showed them how to get back on the road when they had taken a wrong turn. What was it? How did it work?

It was the Spirit of God, the Holy Spirit. God has given us this amazing road atlas and guidebook, the Bible. But because the road you travel is never exactly the same as anyone else's, and because the conditions on your journey are changing from minute to minute, God gives us his Spirit as the ultimate in-body navigation aid. More far-seeing than any human information system could possibly be, more powerful than any computer, wiser than all the world's experts put together, the Holy Spirit speaks quietly to our spirit to guide us in the best possible way.

Jesus explained this to his disciples on the night before he was crucified. He put it like this:

**If you love me, you will do the things I command. I will
ask the Father, and he will give you another Helper.
He will give you this Helper to be with you for ever.
The Helper is the Spirit of truth. The world cannot
accept him because it does not see him or know him.
But you know him. He lives with you and will be in
you.** *John 14:15–17*

He is the "Spirit of truth" — so he never makes a mistake
and sends you in the wrong direction. (Sometimes,
though, he sends you down some roads that seem pretty
strange until you get to the end of them.) He "will be in
you" and "will be with you for ever" — he is always
installed; you can't lose him or forget and leave him
behind. "The world . . . does not see him or know him" —
many people have little idea about spiritual things so they
can't understand the Holy Spirit. But the followers of Jesus
will understand.

And this in-body navigation "helper" is free. In fact, he is
provided by the Boss. To all who love Jesus and want to
live as his followers, Jesus promised: **"I will ask the
Father, and he will give you another Helper."**

Can you travel your journey of life without him?

23
The gourd seed

Theme

Growth and fruit in the Christian life come from being rooted in Jesus. This lesson begins in the spring and continues to harvest. Cyberspace kids need the experience of growing plants to understand the many biblical metaphors drawn from the natural world.

You will need

- enough gourd seeds and plant pots for each child; compost (preferably peat-free); cling film; dust sheets to protect table and floor as necessary.
- card to make growth records.

Presentation

Have a seed-sowing session, giving the children as much explanation as necessary. Moisten the compost and cover the pot with cling film. Tell the children to take the pots home and keep them in a warm room — but not too hot — with a piece of paper over the top. Check every day. When the green sprout shows, remove the film and paper, and place the pot on a window ledge. When the plant is established and all danger of frost has passed, they can plant it out in the garden in a sunny spot. Keep well watered.

The seed that they have planted is able to grow as much as six metres (20 feet) in a year, bearing beautiful fruits that are all kinds of shapes and colours. Some look like pears, or apples, or cucumbers, or melons — and they have a wonderful texture. On one occasion a plant grew from beneath a child's window on the ground, right up past his bedroom window, growing just short of eight metres (25 feet) high.

Good fruit

The intention is to report week by week on its growth, and to point out that if the plant is well watered and well fed, it will grow longer and stronger and have more fruit, just like us. The Bible says that good fruit comes from good trees, and good trees need deep roots. When Paul wrote to the Christians in a town called Colosse, he told them:

> **As you received Christ Jesus the Lord, so continue to live in him. Keep your roots deep in him and have your lives built on him.** *Colossians 2:6–7a*

Paul is using the idea of a growing plant as a picture to encourage us to stay close to Jesus day by day.

Encourage the children to measure their plants week by week, and report back. The children can make a card with the verse above written on it, and a grid to record weekly growth. In the autumn they can bring all their fruit and create an autumn display at Harvest Festival. It is something for the children to look forward to, a lesson to be learned right throughout the year, and one that they can be reminded about at the Harvest Festival service.

Follow-up ideas

Training

If it is just allowed to grow where it likes, the gourd vine can get into places where it should not be, perhaps where it can get damaged. With stakes, string or trellis it can be trained. Draw the parallel with the prodigal son when he went off wherever he wanted. Discipline helps us get more out of life.

Care

Regular watering is essential in dry weather. Feeding helps produce more fruit. Use the children's successes and failures to draw out the lessons. See if they can make the link themselves between regular care for their plant and regular attendance at their Christian group.

24
Open your presents

Theme

Paul's list of gifts that are a blessing to others in Romans 12.

You will need

- to spend an hour in a store and buy lots of small things to wrap as parcels to give out. (Because this works well with adults present and you need a gift for every child, this is best in a church service or, for example, an all-age party. It could be used at Christmas.)

Presentation

Greet people at the door and give out the parcels, asking people not to unwrap them yet. Know your parcels, so that, for example, a bald man gets one containing a comb or a duster.

Come the time for your talk, you could first check if it is anyone's birthday and ask them about their presents.

Now today, you want lots of people to have presents even when it isn't their birthday. Get people to open their presents one at a time and show everybody what they have received. Some mischievous thought in advance (as in the comb for the bald man or bird-seed for the choir "canary") can create some laughter here. Where possible, have the recipients use the gifts straight away. Ask them not to screw up the wrapping paper but to keep it, as you are going to use it later.

Read **Romans 12:6–8**. Better, have a group of children prepare it so that different voices come in for each of the sentences beginning, **"If one has the gift of . . ."**

Draw the distinction between the presents you have given out — things — and the gifts Paul is talking about — abilities, qualities, the kind of person we are. And these are not the sort of things we learn in school. You don't get a GCSE in prophecy or an A-level in encouraging others. You can be totally useless at maths but absolutely brilliant at showing kindness to others. Which rates most highly in God's eyes?

Paul emphasizes that whatever gifts we have, it is vital to use them, to practise them. Ask for a child who learns a musical instrument or a particular sport, and find out how much time they practise each week.

Something to do

Ask people to think about their own gifts, which may or may not be included in this list of Paul's. To help them think, reread Romans 12:6–8.

Get people to take a small piece of wrapping paper and imagine they are wrapping their gift in it. It only makes a tiny, flat parcel, but it is actually much bigger than anything we might get for birthday or Christmas. If it is used, it will go on blessing people — making them happy, thankful, joyful — for as long as you live.

Ask people to hold their tiny parcel in their hand and to pray a quiet prayer thanking God for it and promising to use it.

NOTE

Whatever you do, don't follow the example of a certain vicar who collected the gifts from the children at the end of the service so they could be used another time!

25
Be perfect

Theme

Perfection is both achievable and desirable — with God.

You will need

* to arrange in advance for three or four children to think
  about something perfect in whatever their particular sphere
  of enthusiasm is. For example, one child could think of the
  line-up for the perfect football team, another the
  specifications for the perfect computer set-up, another a
  plan for a perfect day out.

Presentation

Get each of the children who thought about their idea of
perfection to talk about it to the rest of the group. Ask
each whether their idea is realistically possible, given
enough money or other resources. Would it be something
they would actually like to create, perhaps when they are
older, if they had the chance?

We've thought about the perfect computer (or whatever);
how about the perfect "you" — the perfect *Peter* or *Ann* or
Wayne? Is such a thing possible?

The children might like to suggest ways in which they
could become closer to perfection, but don't push this if it
is likely to cause embarrassment or unkind comments
from others.

Now imagine for a moment that God is looking at you.
He is looking at you as you are, but in his mind's eye he
is seeing the perfect *Peter*. And, of course, the perfect
Peter is the one who is capable of both imagining and

creating the perfect computer (or whatever that child's idea was).

Two questions. First: Is that what God wants? Does he want the perfect "you"? What do you think? . . .

In his famous "Sermon on the Mount" Jesus said,

> **You must be perfect, just as your Father in heaven is perfect.** *Matthew 5:48*

So that settles that. God wants the perfect *Peter*.

Second question: Can God do it? Can he make you perfect? . . .

When *the angel Gabriel* came to Mary to tell her she was going to carry the baby Jesus he said to her,

> **Nothing is impossible with God.** *Luke 1:37*

Notice that the angel said, "*with* God". God is capable of doing anything he wants to, but he has given us the free choice of whether we want to work with him or go our own way and do our own thing.

Actually, Jesus would never have said, **"You must be perfect"**, unless it was really possible. Jesus would never ask us to do anything that was impossible.

Another question: What does being perfect mean? Is it being a goody-goody who everyone thinks is a pain in the neck? . . .

Full of possibilities

When you imagine your perfect football team or your perfect computer or your perfect day out, it isn't a pain in the neck, is it? It's exciting. It's full of possibilities. It's something you want to talk about and show others. It's something to be proud of.

And when God imagined you before the creation of the world, he imagined a "you" — a *Peter* or an *Ann* or whoever you are — a "you" who would be an exciting person to be with. He imagined a "you" full of possibilities. He imagined a "you" who would be, not a goody-goody, but a force for good in a messed-up world. He imagined a "you" he would want to talk about and be proud of.

But he didn't just *imagine* you. God has the power to make his dreams come true. So he *created* you and placed you in his extraordinary world.

So each one of us has a choice. We can say, "Wow! I want to be that perfect 'me' that God imagined before the universe was made. I want to explore that full range of gifts and abilities that he designed in me. I want to be a force for good in the world. I want to be fully ready for all those unimaginable possibilities that he is planning for me in the life after this life."

Or we can say, "No, thank you. I'm happy as I am. I'll do it my way."

The choice is yours.

26
Fruitful or poisonous?

Theme

We often talk about the fruit of the Spirit but ignore the contrasting list of destructive attitudes that Paul gives us just before in Galatians chapter five. Here we underline the fact that you can't have the one without first dealing with the other.

You will need

- a selection of fresh fruits; one or two tins of fruit with the labels removed; paper to wrap them each in; tin-opener, spoons and blindfolds.
- nine cards, each with an example of the "fruit of the Spirit" written on them, as listed in **Galatians 5:22–23**.

Presentation

Produce the wrapped fruits one at a time and ask some children to guess what each one is by feeling it. A banana is obvious, but an apple and an orange can be confused. As for the tins, that is sheer guesswork! When unwrapped, they are still a mystery, as the labels have been removed.

Have one or two children blindfolded and see if they can guess the contents of a tin by taste. If one contains something like lychees this can be quite a test.

We normally do not have a problem recognizing common types of fruit when we see them. If we can't see them it can be more difficult. They still taste good, though! (Well, maybe lychees aren't to everyone's taste.) And they certainly do us good. People who eat a lot of fruit tend to live longer than those who don't.

St Paul wrote about a different kind of fruit, the fruit of the Spirit. Have nine children come out and hold the prepared cards with the blank side to the audience. Like the fruit wrapped in paper or hidden in tins, these types of fruit can't be seen. They are hidden inside people.

See how many of them the children know. Turn each one round as it is remembered or guessed.

Although they are hidden inside people, that doesn't mean to say we can't recognize them quite easily. We just need to be around people long enough to see whether they have patience or kindness or self-control. (The children with the cards can now sit down.)

A poisonous sort of person

Just a bit before this, Paul gives another list. It contains things like: hating, making trouble, being jealous, being angry, being selfish, making people angry with each other. Someone like that would be a pretty poisonous sort of person. Would you like to spend time around a person who was like that inside? Would you like to *be* a person who was like that?

St Paul tells us how we get from being that kind of poisonous person to being someone who has the wonderful fruit of the Spirit growing in them:

> **Those who belong to Christ Jesus have crucified their own sinful selves. They have given up their old selfish feelings and the evil things they wanted to do. We get our new life from the Spirit. So we should follow the Spirit.** *Galatians 5:24–25*

If we have a bush in the garden that grows poisonous fruit, the only thing to do is to dig it up and throw it in the bin. It is dangerous to have around. If we look inside ourselves and see things like hating, making trouble, being jealous, being angry, or being selfish, the only thing to do is to say: "The 'me' that does those poisonous things has got to go. I don't want to be like that any more. I am a danger to myself and others."

A prayer

Then we need the courage to pray like this:

Lord Jesus, you died on the cross to deal with poisonous stuff like that. So please deal with that sinful me. Let it be crucified with you. Help me to give up the old selfish feelings. And Lord Jesus, give me a new life from the Spirit. Change me from the inside so that the good fruit, the wonderful fruit, grows in me. Amen.

Have a time of quiet reflection and give the opportunity for anyone who prayed like that, or would like to pray like that, to talk to a leader.

NOTE

A wonderful illustration of this is the story of David Lant in "Light from behind bars", p. 69. It would make a good follow-up.

27
Through and through

Theme

Knowing Jesus releases the energy of his love to work in us and through us.

You will need

* a number of sticks of rock with "Jesus" written all the way through. These can be obtained in Britain by phoning 01909 476414 (or worldwide by logging onto the website). Keep one or more whole, and cut enough pieces for each child to have one.

Presentation

If you see the children before the holiday period, ask them to bring back a stick of rock from the place they have been to on holiday, or one with their own name in it. The latter are widely available.

Ask some children to bring their rock and tell you a little about their holiday, and how they remembered to buy the rock, and where they got it from. (Children have been known to insist on buying the stick of rock before they do anything else on holiday.) Memories of holidays are good, and a stick of rock with the name of the place all the way through is a nice reminder.

Rock with our name all the way through is fun, although most of us don't need a stick of rock to remind us who we are — certain ageing leaders excepted!

Show your Jesus rock and get a child to read the name in it. Give every child a piece so that they can all see the name — and suck it slowly while you go on talking.

Read Ephesians 3:17 and 19. In this letter Paul says,

I pray that Christ will live in your hearts because of your faith. I pray that your life will be strong in love and be built on love . . . Christ's love is greater than any person can ever know. But I pray that you will be able to know that love. Then you can be filled with all the fullness of God.

As we suck a piece of rock, we are dissolving the sugar, which will be absorbed into our bodies and give us energy. But when we believe in Jesus, a far greater power comes into us. Jesus himself lives in our innermost being, our "heart", and the more we open our lives to him, the more his love fills us.

More than we can think of

That love is so great that it is beyond human understanding. But Paul prays that we can know it — feel it, experience it.

If you have a heart to change the world, then you need a heart filled with the love of Jesus. The sugar in this rock will give us the energy to run around for an hour or so. That's nothing compared to the power of the love of Jesus in us. The next verse in this letter says,

With God's power working in us, God can do much, much more than anything we can ask or think of.

Knowing Jesus releases the energy of his love to work in us and through us. That's a power that will last your whole life long.

Let's listen to the whole of Paul's prayer. If we want, as we listen, we can ask God to make this real for us so that the love of Jesus fills us through and through — like his name through this stick of rock.

A prayer

Read **Ephesians 3:17–21** as a prayer.

28
Unimaginable power

Theme

The incredible power of God's kingdom is right at hand.

You will need

- a battery; some electrically powered items; some balloons.

Presentation

If working with families, ask a father to pick up a child and *vice versa*. With children only, get one child first to pick up something light, then to try something impossibly heavy. (Make sure it really is too heavy, not something the child might attempt to pick up and strain himself.)

Why can't *John* pick up *his dad*? . . . Because he's too heavy. In other words, because of gravity. The force of gravity is what keeps us all stuck to the ground. It's what makes sure that when our ice-cream falls out of the cornet it hits the ground, not a pigeon flying overhead!

I want to tell you about another force. It's not a million times stronger than gravity. It's not a billion times stronger. It's a billion billion billion billion times stronger! Pow! That sounds like dangerous stuff! It is — and yet it is what is holding you together right now. It's the glue that holds every atom in your body together — it's called the electrical force. It keeps the electrons buzzing around the nucleus in every atom.

Let's see what happens when we knock a few electrons off something. We've all done this.

Rub a balloon on a sweater and stick it to a wall. Hold another near a child's face so she can feel the hairs being attracted by the balloon.

One in a billion billion

What we've done here is to knock off a few electrons from the surface of the balloon. Just one in a billion billion electrons releases enough force to make this balloon defy gravity. If you find a way of knocking more electrons off, then you can do something really useful. For example, you can use chemicals and make a battery. And that battery can power a torch, or an electronic game, or a mobile phone.

The power company Powergen does it differently. They use huge generators to create mains electricity, which powers our lights, vacuum cleaner, TV, etc.

If you went home today and had no electricity, what couldn't you do? . . . Imagine life without it! Yet for most of human history, people didn't even know it existed. Only in 1752 did Benjamin Franklin fly a kite in a thunderstorm and demonstrate the existence of electricity. (Don't try it — you could kill yourself.) And it was much later that electricity companies started to connect houses. Some people didn't want to be connected. They preferred to stick to candles and gas-lights. Imagine!

But this isn't supposed to be a science lesson. So what's it got to do with God? Well, when Jesus started going round preaching his message was:

> **Good news! Turn around. The kingdom of the heavens is very close to you.** *Cf. Matthew 4:17, Mark 1:15*

"The kingdom of the heavens" — or God's kingdom — what's that? Where is it?

Plugged into reality

Well, it's something like this. [Hold up the battery.] We can't see the electrons, but we know that when we connect the battery up, something happens. The kingdom of the heavens is like that. Only it's fantastically more powerful than even the electrical force. Jesus started to show people what he was talking about. He says a word and: Pow! — a blind man sees . . . Pow! — a lame man walks . . . Pow! — a picnic lunch feeds a huge crowd . . . Pow! — a leper is healed . . . Pow! — tax-collectors give up cheating people . . . That's the power of the kingdom of the heavens. It's a new way of living. It's a way of plugging into real truth, real goodness, real love.

It's like the electrical force — but it's personal. You get plugged in by knowing God as your Father through Jesus.

It's like the electrical force — but it's trillions of times stronger. This is the power that created the whole universe! You can't get any bigger than that. And yet it's close. So close you can touch it. It's as close as believing in Jesus and saying, "Yes, I want to swap my old life for this new kingdom life."

You can't see the kingdom of the heavens? No, but you can see schools and hospitals and care for children and a thousand things that were started by people who were plugged into the kingdom. Lots of people in the world don't want to get connected to God's kingdom? OK, but some people didn't want to connect their houses up to the electric power lines, either. Some people just don't know a good thing when they see it!

A prayer

Lord God, King of all creation, teach us more about the wonders and the power of your kingdom. We often pray, "Your kingdom come" — please show us how the power of your kingdom can make that true in our lives and in the world around us. Amen.

29
Power in action

Theme

The story of the poor widow giving all she had is an example of kingdom power in action. This talk follows on from "Unimaginable power"; the two can be presented as one longer all-age message.

You will need

- a power tool; two small coins; a bag of coins or a cheque for a large amount; enough smallest denomination coins to give two to each person.

Presentation

Ask the children questions to review the teaching in "Unimaginable power".

People who have learned about living in the kingdom of the heavens are different. Jesus pointed out one of them just a few days before he was crucified.

Tell the story in **Mark 12:41–44** of the poor widow putting all she had into the temple offering box. Use the coins and cheque to illustrate the story. Tell the children that there were no benefits or social security, so that as a widow this woman would have no income.

Jesus said:

> **This poor woman has put more into the collection than all the others.**

More than all the others? What did Jesus mean? How can these two tiny coins be worth more than this bag of silver/cheque?

Well, we might say, she put in all she had, so in proportion to what she owned she gave more than the others. Is that what Jesus means? Maybe. But Jesus said,

she really gave more than all those rich people.

Could what she gave really be worth more than the large sums the rich people put in? How?

Think about what we have learned about God's power, the power of the kingdom of the heavens. This woman's heart attitude shows that she was plugged into God's kingdom. So her giving was like pressing the switch.

A tiny action

Demonstrate with a power tool. A tiny action pressing the switch releases power that enables a handyman to drill holes in concrete or saw through thick planks of wood. (Be sure to unplug the power tool as soon as you finish using it and put it out of reach of small hands.)

If the attitude of the heart is right, what may seem to be only a very small thing releases kingdom power, the power of God. We don't know what happened as a result of the faith and generosity of that widow, except that it was recorded in the Bible and countless millions of people have heard the story and been affected by it.

This story shows us that kingdom power is not for people who want to show off by the miracles they perform. It is for those who are humble and trusting and faithful. And you need the eyes of Jesus to see that power being switched on and to see what it achieves.

Something to do

Give everyone two small coins. Ask them to keep the coins in their pocket as a reminder of this story. Suggest that as the children feel the coins from time to time, they ask God to show them some small act of kindness or generosity that they can do. This is not to boast about or to show what nice people we are, but we pray it can come out of a loving and trusting heart.

NOTE

Alternatively, you can give the coins out at the start. This creates a bit of intrigue and the children can have them in their hands as you are telling the story.

Ingredients for a Healthy Lifestyle

Listen to the Creator to
get the best out of life

30
Proof of the pudding

Theme

The most important ingredients of a good life are in Paul's list of the fruit of the Spirit.

You will need

- a microwave cooker, extension lead if needed, apron, mixing bowl, wooden spoon, 1.2 litre (2 pint) pudding basin, enough teaspoons for large-scale tasting.
- ingredients for a recipe, e.g. 75g (3oz) plain Fair Trade chocolate, 30ml (2tbsp) milk, 175g (6oz) light muscovado sugar, 175g (6oz) margarine, 2 eggs, 175g (6oz) fresh white breadcrumbs, 30ml (2tbsp) cocoa powder.
  a. Melt the chocolate with the milk on High power for 1 minute and mix until smooth.
  b. Mix the sugar and margarine together, then add the cooled chocolate and eggs.
  c. Mix in the breadcrumbs and cocoa powder thoroughly.
  d. Spoon the mixture into the basin. Cook on High power for 6–7 minutes. Leave to stand for 5 minutes before tasting.

Presentation

Get a child to come and help you make a chocolate pudding. Dress him or her in an apron and a chef's hat if you can get hold of one. (Hotels sometimes use paper ones and will let you have one if you ask.) You could stage this like a current TV cooking programme for extra topicality.

Get the child to mix the ingredients and keep up a running commentary. Place in the microwave and leave to cook. Thank the child — with a promise that he or she can come back and have the first taste when it is ready.

Cooking is fun, but you need to have the right ingredients. Of course, when you get a bit knowledgeable about cooking, you can experiment. Keeping the basic recipe, we could have made a pudding with currants in instead of chocolate. Does anyone have any other suggestions? . . .

Life needs the right ingredients, too. St Paul gives a list of wonderful ingredients in his letter to the churches in Galatia (modern Turkey): love, joy, peace, patience, kindness, goodness, faithfulness, gentleness, self-control (Galatians 5:22). There is no way a life with these ingredients could be a disaster!

There are many other possible ingredients and, because each one of us is a unique and special person, every life will be different. You can add your love of painting, or your knowledge of technology, or your ability to swim 50 lengths. The important thing is to get the basic ingredients right. Where do you get them?

A litre of patience?

You can't buy a kilo of love, or a tin of peace, or a litre of patience. So where do they come from? St Paul said, **"The Spirit gives love, joy, peace,"** and all the rest. That is, the Spirit of God, the Holy Spirit. When someone lives a life close to God, open to God, then the Spirit of God comes to live within that person. And the Spirit just naturally and freely gives you these wonderful ingredients. It is his delight to give them to you.

In fact, Paul even said in another letter that people like this begin to smell good, just like this pudding does! (See 2 Corinthians 2:14–16.) It really pleases God to have people made to this "recipe".

So take a big bowl full of love, joy and peace. Stir in the sweetness of patience, kindness and goodness. Add the finishing touches of faithfulness, gentleness and self-control. And what do you have? A recipe for a life that will fully satisfy you — and be a joy to loads of people you meet in your journey of life.

If the pinger hasn't gone on the microwave yet, then it's time for a song. Be ready with plenty of spoons at the close so that everyone can test out the old adage about the proof of the pudding!

31
The unwinnable prize

Theme

The best prizes in life are things that cannot be won; they can only be received as gifts.

You will need

- questions and props to emulate whatever happens to be the popular quiz show of the moment; cheques (make or print them from the www.77talks.co.uk website); sweets.

Presentation

Run your quiz and give cheques as prizes. The first — lower value — cheques can be swapped for simple prizes, e.g. sweets.

After a few rounds, announce that you are now getting to the big-value prizes. The successful contestant at this point is given a cheque with the word PEACE[1] on it. Your contestant will probably be disappointed, or at least puzzled. Ask why. . . . Is peace not far more valuable than sweets? Wouldn't people in some parts of the world — or those in mental turmoil — give anything for peace?

The child may be smart enough to see the flaw in your argument. If not, help him or her out. Peace is, of course, of far greater value than sweets, but you cannot win peace. Award your contestant a prize in lieu and return the child to the audience.

Produce another cheque, either a giant one that everyone can see, or one drawn on an OHP transparency. It carries these words: **"My peace I give you."**

Right signature

Peace is a gift. You can't win it. But it can be given to you — provided the right signature is on the cheque. Who said this? Jesus. Write *Jesus* on the signature line.

The question is: How much do we believe that signature is worth? How far can we trust it?

Does anyone know when Jesus said this? . . . It was the night before he was crucified, as he shared his last meal with his disciples. They had trusted him enough to give up their jobs and follow him. In the next few hours he was going to be arrested and crucified. As he died a cruel death on a Roman cross it was going to seem that their trust had been in vain. All their hopes would be shattered. How can you have peace in those kind of circumstances?

Yet just 48 hours later, Jesus was going to come back to them. Suddenly, behind locked doors, he would appear. And his very first words? **"Peace be with you!"** (John 20:21) Their trust would be proved right. The gift of peace was real.

Now, who wants to receive this cheque . . . ?

NOTE
1 Other words and appropriate biblical texts can be used to fit in with a particular theme if you wish.

32
Fore! thought

Theme

Keeping our eyes fixed on Jesus.

This talk works best with an all-age group.

You will need

- a set of golf clubs, a golf ball, a table tennis ball, a "hole" (one of the golf aids that is used on a carpet, or create one).
- enough golf tees for everyone to have one (optional, but worthwhile).

Presentation

Talk about how much you enjoy golf and want to get in a bit of practice. Show the golf ball and bounce it very forcibly on the floor, while palming the table tennis ball in your hand. Then place the table tennis ball right out at the front of the hall or church. With care, people will not see that you have swapped balls. Tee up and strike it as straight and hard as you can, keeping your eye very much on the ball and your head still. The congregation will dive for cover before realizing what you have done!

It is probably best not to hack it back out from the pews into the aisle, but rather to ask for the shot to be dropped. You might like to get a child to help with the putting.

As you complete the "hole", stress the importance of two things: knowing exactly where we want to end up — in the hole — and keeping our eye on the ball as we hit it. The first is obvious, but non-golfers are unlikely to be aware of the second.

Many hazards

On the way, there are all sorts of hazards: bunkers, water, trees, even going out of bounds. But if we keep our eye on the ball and keep our mind on what we are doing, we shall get there in the end. Practise enough and you might even become a world-class golfer!

In life we need to have a clear idea of where we want to end up — in that amazing existence called heaven. And the way to get there is to keep our eyes on Jesus. He will always take us through the obstacles and hazards. We may fall into them, but his everlasting arms will be there to lift us out and set us back on the fairway again.

The big difference from golf is that the winner of a round of golf is the one who has the lowest score. On the fairway to heaven, everyone who keeps their eyes fixed on Jesus is a guaranteed winner. There are no losers, and it doesn't matter how long it takes you.

Something to do

Give everyone a golf tee. The golf tee is a reminder that every hole in golf has a beginning and that it has a clear end in view. Get them to hold it while repeating Hebrews 12:2,

Let us keep our eyes fixed on Jesus, on whom our faith depends from beginning to end.

Good News Bible

Ask people to keep the golf tee in their pocket during the week. Every time they feel it, it will be a reminder to look to Jesus.

33
Going for gold

Theme

Picturing a heavenly "medal ceremony" helps motivate us to be the best that we can be.

You will need

- to make three medals or rosettes — gold, silver and bronze — fixing £1, 50p and 2p coins in the centre of the appropriate medals.
- items for a race or competition of some kind.

Presentation

Invite all the children to take part in a race, or some of them to take part in another competition depending on the facilities available. This will be more fun if they are competing against you or other leaders, especially if the sport is chosen to ensure that children will win.

Hold a medal ceremony. If you can play this up with anthems and flowers, so much the better. The winners can remove and keep the coins.

Athletes who aim for the top get into serious training. Cyclocross champion, Rob Dane, for example, the number two in the world, cycles 50–65,000 kilometres (30–40,000 miles) every year in training. Today's Olympic games continue a tradition that goes back to ancient Greece. At the time when Paul was writing the letters we have in the New Testament, the Isthmian games were held in Corinth every three years. Athletes would go into ten months of strict training to prepare for the games.

Your life's ambition

Very few of us have what it takes physically or mentally to reach the highest level in sport. But that doesn't mean that we can't "go for gold". Imagine for a moment a vast stadium, a stadium so big that it can hold the entire population of the world. The whole place is bathed in a wonderful golden light. Imagine that there is a podium in the middle of that arena and that you are standing on it. A shimmering figure approaches and you bend forward to receive, not a medal, but a gold crown. The whole stadium erupts in cheering and clapping. You lift your hands to acknowledge the cheers, feeling both very big and very small at the same time. Your eyes fill with tears of joy, knowing you have achieved your life's ambition.

Fantasy? Not for Paul and other New Testament writers who used images like this to give us a glimpse of the future. Writing about life to people in Corinth (where the Isthmian games were held), Paul said,

> **Run to win! All those who compete in the games use strict training. They do this so that they can win a crown. That crown is an earthly thing [actually a pine wreath] that lasts only a short time. But our crown will continue for ever.** *1 Corinthians 9:25*

What does it take to fulfill that dream and win a crown that lasts for ever? Simple: be yourself! Be the person that God created you to be, but be that to the best you can possibly be.

A phone company put out a TV ad that showed a vast stadium like the one we have been imagining — created inside a computer, of course. In the ad, different people stand in the arena to talk about their ideas or dreams or inventions. A young mum holds her baby and says she sometimes feels overwhelmed by the responsibility and scared that she won't be able to cope. She asks if anyone else ever feels like that.

Being real

The camera turns to a section of the crowd full of mums and babies. One by one they nod and begin to stand. A wave ripples up the stadium as thousands of mums rise to show they all feel like that at times. The mum in the middle was being real, being honest, being herself. And the viewer watching the ad knows that she will find it easier to cope because now she knows she is not alone. All young mums feel overwhelmed by the responsibility of that young life in their arms.

At times in our lives, running to win simply means being as good a mum or as good a dad as we can be — with God's help. Or as good a student, or as good a friend as we can be — with God's help. At times we may be involved in, say, a project to help people in need. We can give our best to that — with God's help. At other times in our lives, we may get a sense of being called to do something or be something special. Paul was called by God to take the good news of Jesus to dozens of towns like Corinth in the Roman empire. But God has as many different things for people to do as there are people.

Going for gold — doing things to the best of our possibilities — is tough at times. A mum knows she cannot take a day off and just leave her baby in the cot. Athletes know that you can't let up on the training. Paul talked about training like a boxer — even hitting his own body and giving himself a black eye! (1 Corinthians 9:26–27) — as a picture of his determination to spread the amazing story of Jesus and his resurrection round the world.

132

Something to do

Close your eyes and think of something you are involved in at the moment — a situation with a friend or within your family, a skill you are learning, a project or an adventure you are planning, a difficult challenge you are facing. Thank God for the resources you have to face this challenge and ask him to help you see it through. Ask him to make you tough — the kind of person who doesn't give up and give in. And imagine that scene in the stadium again. Imagine yourself on the podium, receiving that everlasting gold crown. Imagine how good that feels. Go for it!

Note: during this meditation it would be good to play some music in the background, eg a piece associated with a major sporting event being broadcast on television.

34
Curried grapefruit

Theme

We may look very different and act differently, but we are all one in Jesus, the bread of life.

You will need

- to make up some sandwiches with odd fillings, e.g. chicken and banana, beetroot and jelly beans, curried grapefruit (made with spicy chutney), liquorice and sardines, or whatever unlikely combinations you can come up with. Alternatively, do the same with pizza toppings.

Presentation

Find out who eats sandwiches and what their favourite fillings are (or pizzas and favourite toppings).

Now you need some adventurous characters who are willing to taste samples of a new range which you think could go down really big.

Give your volunteers your prepared concoctions and ask them if they can say what the fillings are. Provide a basin to spit into, and water for those who need to wash the taste away!

The followers of Jesus come in all sorts of shapes, sizes and weird combinations. His first disciples were a pretty motley bunch. They wore what many of us would think of as strange clothes; at least one was a tax-collector — a traitor working for the enemy — and several of them probably smelled rather strongly of fish!

Some were barbarians

As belief in Jesus spread, all kinds of people began to discover this new life, a life with the power and love of Jesus in them. They spoke different languages, ate different kinds of food, had different customs. In those early days, some were free citizens of the Roman empire and some were slaves. Some were highly educated and civilized; some were barbarians. But it wasn't the differences that mattered any longer; it was what they all shared.

In one of his letters, Paul reminded people about this,

> **In the new life there is no difference between Greeks and Jews. There is no difference between those who are circumcised and those who are not circumcised, or people that are foreigners, or Scythians [the most barbarous barbarians]. There is no difference between slaves and free people. But Christ is in all believers. And Christ is all that is important.** *Colossians 3:11*

It's not the filling that matters. It's the bread. And Jesus once called himself **"the bread of life"**. (John 6:35)

Get one child to stand on a chair and look down on the others.

One of the easiest temptations to give way to is to look down on other people because they are different. Whether it's the clothes they wear or the food they eat or the music they like, we can kid ourselves into thinking that they are inferior and we are superior.

A new kind of life

But Jesus brought a new kind of life. And people who get into this new life discover that they are on the same level as everyone else. (Get the child to sit down again.)

At least, they *should* discover that. Sadly, some Christians don't get the message and even think that they are superior because their church is better than other churches!

Differences can be fun. (We can learn to laugh at ourselves.) Differences can be interesting. Differences can teach us things we didn't know and help us discover new experiences. But the really important thing is what we share: Jesus, the bread of life.

A prayer

In the same bit of that letter Paul said,

> **In your new life you are being made new. You are becoming like the One who made you.**
>
> *Colossians 3:10*

It doesn't happen all at once. We are being changed bit by bit to become more like Jesus. So perhaps we can pray something like this:

> **Lord Jesus, when we start to feel superior, may your Holy Spirit give us a nudge and remind us that in your sight we are all equal. And when we feel inferior, remind us that you are in us, the bread of life, and that nobody can look down on you. Amen.**

35
Trousers three times as risky as skirts

Theme

Home accident statistics lead into considering the risks Jesus pointed out in the parable of the house built on sand.

You will need

- a box, a lump of cheese, a pair of socks, a sandwich, a slipper, a magazine.
- if possible, a hard-hat, goggles and gloves.
- other items from the talk as desired.

Presentation

This is a good introduction for ham actors! Announce that today you are going to be thinking about safety education and you have brought in some dangerous items. Put on protective clothing if you have it, then gingerly produce items as above from the box.

All these items landed people in hospital, according to government figures on safety in the home. Every year, the government produces a report based on people who end up in the Accident and Emergency unit at 18 of the country's largest hospitals.[1] Multiplying the numbers from those hospitals to give us a picture of the whole country, it looks like in one year, no less than 957 people were injured by cheese, while sandwiches accounted for 4,472 cases needing a doctor's attention!

Slippers turn out to be nearly 14 times as dangerous as wellington boots. So if you know someone who puts on slippers when they get home from work, warn them of the risks and tell them to wear wellies round the house instead. Better to be safe than sorry! And as for trainers, 27,752 accidents were caused by them. As only 234 injuries were caused by clogs, quite clearly people who go out for an early morning jog should run in clogs. (Does anyone know if Reebok does a line in high-tech clogs?)

As for the 8,593 injuries caused by socks or tights, the mind boggles! How do you injure yourself on a pair of socks? Is it possible that some people's socks smell so strongly that they pass out when getting undressed, hitting their heads on the dressing table as they fall?

One of the most enlightening categories is injuries caused by office and school equipment. You might think that sharp-pointed compasses or dividers posed the worst threat. But no. In fact, they only accounted for 20 accidents, far fewer than the 488 caused by seemingly harmless crayons. The really dangerous school items turn out to be *pens, pencils, paper and books* — running up a worrying 11,054 injuries between them!

Does this mean there ought to be a nationwide schoolkids' strike, demanding the banning of books, pens and paper in schools? All in the interests of safety, of course! (But before anyone gets too tempted, you ought to know that far more injuries were caused by footballs.)

All this goes to show that you never know when disaster may strike. It's not just that the unexpected may happen at any time; it's *how* unexpected the unexpected is. At least now you've been warned that any time you put your socks on, you risk ending up in Accident and Emergency.

The reason the government collects these figures is so that they can spot increases in accidents related to different items, and run campaigns warning people of the dangers. Forewarned is forearmed, so they say.

There's a well-known story designed to forewarn people of danger. It's a story not so much of an accident *in* the home as an accident *to* the home. It goes like this:

Read or tell the story in **Matthew 7:24–27**. This is how Jesus ends his crucial teaching about everyday life that we call the Sermon on the Mount.

Something to think about

An accident can change the course of your life. A disaster can end it. Jesus was saying, "If you want to avoid a certain kind of disaster in your life, listen to my teaching and put it into practice. Don't end up as one of life's casualties."

NOTE

1 All information taken from the Department of Trade and Industry's *Home Accident Surveillance System* (HASS data) for 1998.

36
Are we blind?

Theme

The dangers of taking something when we are not sure of what it is or what it might do to us.

You will need

- a blindfold, a piece of fruit, a small packet of sweets.
- a plastic "doggy-doo" from a joke shop.

Presentation

Ask for three volunteers to play a guessing game. Explain the rules: You are going to blindfold them one at a time, and ask them to hold out one hand, palm flat. An object will be placed on the outstretched palm. They must not close their fingers to feel it — appoint a referee to watch. They can ask you eight "yes or no" questions about the object (five if time is short). Each time the answer is "yes", they can have one guess as to what it is. Give a prize (or keep the object) for the correct answer.

The first two objects — fruit and sweets — are straightforward. The third is the "doggy-doo". This will occasion a lot of mirth in the audience — and revulsion when the contestant finds out what he is holding.

Heroin re-branded

Thank the volunteers, and continue in this vein: Are we sometimes blind to what people are offering us?

For example, a study has shown that young people can be tricked into taking heroin, thinking it is a less harmful, "recreational" drug. Dealers can "re-brand" heroin and sell it in affordable, small bags. Sometimes they give it a different name.

The average age of users has dropped from 17–25 to 14–25. Children as young as ten to twelve years old have been found smoking and injecting the drug. Many are completely ignorant of the addictive powers of the Class A drug.

Talk about the dangers of taking "blind" anything that is offered to us. This could apply to tablets, or drink, or videos. Reinforce the message with the "doggy-doo" and the difficulties of cleaning ourselves up once we have been fouled.

37
Who's in control?

Theme

A warning about those who try to control us, and a discussion of the virtue of self-control.

You will need

- Watch some prime-time TV and take a note of the slogans or punch lines of a number of advertisements. Prepare a list of these with key words missing.

Presentation

Either read out the ads and get everyone to call out the missing words, or make a bit more of it by recruiting two teams and running it as a quiz. (With a mixed-age group you will be chastened to note that children not long out of nappies will be able to do this.) Small prizes appropriate to one of the ads might be offered.

A successful advertising campaign is one that gets us to remember either a product name, or a slogan associated with a product. Of course, it costs a lot of money to run a major campaign. Car manufacturers, soft drinks companies, brewers, sportswear companies . . . these are some of the groups that spend millions of pounds trying to sell us an image that they want us to buy into.

Someone has written, **"The rich are always trying to control your lives."** We can see the truth of that every day on our TV screens. Rich companies can afford the best ideas people, the best directors and actors to make their ads, the best prime-time TV slots.

Influencing our thoughts

Their aim is to influence the way we think about ourselves and other people, and how we spend our money. In other words, they are trying to control our lives. We watch the ads, we buy the products — and the directors of the companies pay themselves huge salaries and retire with millions of pounds in the bank.

"The rich are always trying to control your lives." (James 2:6) That is bang up to date, but it was written nearly 2,000 years ago. It was James, probably the brother of Jesus, who wrote it in a letter to Christians all over the world.

It wasn't the only thing he had to say about the rich. He gave them a dire warning, too:

> **You rich people, listen! Cry and be very sad because of the troubles that are coming to you. Your riches have rotted, and your clothes have been eaten by moths. Your gold and silver have rusted, and that rust will be a proof that you were wrong. It will eat your bodies like fire. You saved your treasure for the last days. Men worked in your fields but you did not pay them. They harvested your crops and are crying out against you. Now the Lord of heaven's armies has heard their cries.** *James 5:1–4*

The pay-packets may be big, but if James is right, the future is not too bright for the rich who are trying to control our lives.

Something to think about

Two of James' fellow leaders of the early church, Peter and Paul, urge us to be *self*-controlled. Self-control means stopping to think about what we do and why. It means deciding for ourselves how we spend our money, rather than letting rich companies do the thinking for us.

How often do we make fun of someone or call them names because they don't have the "right" trainers or the "right" brand of trousers or soft drinks or whatever? Whenever we do that we are playing right into the hands of the rich companies, strengthening the control they have over people's lives, doing their dirty work for them.

So how about starting a revolution? It's a revolution in which respect goes to the people who think for themselves. Respect for people who don't buy the big-name clothes because they don't want to make the fat cats fatter. Respect for people who can laugh at the ads but not get taken in by them.

It's a revolution that needs self-control. Get on board, because self-control equals self-respect. That's got to be better than allowing the rich to control our lives.

38
Sniff for success

Theme

How to please God — and not create a stink.

You will need

- a bottle of fragrance such as those widely available for aromatherapy or to put onto potpourri. Choose an unusual fragrance and spread enough around the room to make sure it is obvious to everyone as they enter.
- if possible, some incense and a censer, as used in some churches.

Presentation

No, I've not had an accident with the after-shave or eau de toilette. This is essential oil of . . . [whatever — show bottle].

This is a serious tip for helping study for tests or exams or for learning that part in the Christmas play.

It has long been known that smells can call up memories of things that happened a long time in the past. (You could talk about something that brings back a memory for you.) Psychologists have shown that smells can also help you learn facts and remember them when you come to take a test.

You need something a little unusual. Perfume the room you are working in while you are revising or trying to learn something by heart. Then, on the day of the test or exam, have a drop on a handkerchief so that you can sniff it.

Anxious about tests?

Research done by Dr Rachel Herz in Philadelphia[1] showed that volunteers using perfume like this were able to remember almost 20% more of the words they were given to learn for a test. It actually works better if you are the kind of person who normally gets rather anxious when it comes to tests.

In Old Testament times, when the Israelites brought some grain or cakes to offer as a sacrifice, part of it was mixed with oil and incense and burned on the altar. Incense is a mixture of gum and spices which gives off a sweet smell when burned.

Demonstrate, if you have incense.

This part that was burned was known as the "memorial portion" (see Leviticus 2:1–10). The smell was said to be pleasing to God, and this was a way of asking God to "remember" the worshipper.

The idea of God being pleased by a smell might seem rather primitive to us, but it shows that even then, people were well aware of the link between smell and memory.

They also knew the importance of being right with God. That meant bringing something of value and offering it as a sacrifice to God, and doing it in the best way they knew how, including making it smell good.

Christians today believe that when Jesus died on the cross, he offered himself as a once-and-for-all sacrifice, and that now we can approach God through him.

So when we do something wrong — something that "stinks" — we can ask forgiveness. In this way, Christians rejoice that God only remembers the good in their lives, and not the stinks they have created.

Something to do

How about trying this with a Bible verse or two in your church or group? Learn the passage one week and see how people do at recalling it — with fragrant assistance — a week later.

NOTE

1 Reported in *The Psychologist*, November 1997.

39
A winning combination

Theme

A football illustration provides a talk based on Proverbs 20:29 — "The glory of young men is their strength; of old men, their experience."

You will need

- up-to-date information about the current star players and managers.

Presentation

A football enthusiast could be asked to prepare a report on a match, or you could begin with news of the latest sacking or appointing of a manager.

Our heroes are usually the young men — or women — on the pitch [such as . . .]. But equally important to the team's success is the manager. The manager has often been a successful player himself. He has had experience of the game, can analyze tactics, see players' strengths and weaknesses, and judge how to combine those strengths to build a team that is strong both in attack and defence.

He needs to be able to communicate effectively to the players so that they can understand the team strategy and tactics. He needs to be able to motivate them to give of their best (usually referred to in soccer as the mythical 110%).

Although they did not play soccer 3,000 years ago, King Solomon knew about successful team building. He wrote:

The glory of young men is their strength; of old men, their experience.   *Proverbs 20:29*, The Living Bible

A successful team combines the strengths of young people and the experience of older people.

Although most of us won't ever be professional sportsmen or women, we shall all be part of various "teams". Any group of people tackling a task together is a team. We shall be part of a team when we start work. If we join a club or voluntary organization we shall be part of a team.

Good career move

As young people, what you have to offer the team is your "strength". That can be literally physical strength, or it can be skill, or knowledge, or enthusiasm. What you will not have at first is experience. That can only come with years of doing a job. To be a successful part of the team, you need a good manager — someone who has the experience you lack and who can show you how to get the best out of your strengths.

Any young footballer would want to be part of a team with [current names] as the manager. He would know how much his career would benefit from being under such leadership.

So look for older men and women who are good "managers". When you find them, value their experience, listen to their advice, follow their example. See how much you can learn from them.

Solomon knew a trick or two. **"The glory of young men is their strength; of old men, their experience."** Put the two together and you get a winning combination.

A prayer

Lord God, I want to get the best out of the strengths you have given me. Send me some good managers as I go through life. Help me to recognize them, to listen to them, and to learn from their experience. Amen.

40
Baby talk

Theme

Good advice on how to avoid the mistakes our parents' generation made.

You will need

- copies of the sketch (you can print them out from *www.77talks.co.uk*); two large faces painted onto card (this doesn't have to be great art); a large white towel as a nappy, and appropriate clothes for an outsize baby; the biggest teddy bear you can borrow; a pillow and a sheet or blanket.
- BABY DESMOND can say the words in the script, or they can be voiced over as his thoughts by someone with a microphone.

Presentation

Ask the children what they are looking forward to about growing up. . . . Who is fed up of being a child and would like to grow up quickly? . . . We are going to see someone who is very keen to grow up.

Sketch

A table is covered with a sheet or blanket as a bed. MUM and AUNT BETTY are hidden behind the table with the two large faces and the teddy bear. BABY DESMOND, a leader or older child dressed as a baby, is revealed lying on the bed.

BABY TALK

BABY   (*crying — pause — cries louder*)
MUM   (*first face appears and looks down at BABY*) What's a

matter then, diddums? Who's making a lot of silly-willy noisey. Won't little Dessy-Wessy give his mummy a smile, then?

BABY   The name's Desmond, not Dessy-Wessy. You ought to know, you called me it. I can't stand all this stupid "Dessy-Wessy" business!

MUM   Oh dear, who's not a happy little chap today? Would he like his teddy? Nice cuddles with teddy. Mummy get teddy for Dessy-Wessy.

BABY   Oh no, not the teddy! Watch out, here it comes! Great hairy, ugly thing. It stinks something awful. I just can't wait to grow up. Get off, you great furry brute!

MUM   Little Dessy-Wessy's got a temper on him today, hasn't he diddums? Has he got a pain in his little tummy, then?

BABY   He's got something in his little tummy — and here it comes! *(loud rude noise)*

MUM   Oh dear, he's filled his nappy. Who's a little pooey-pants, then? What a nasty smelly-welly! And just when Aunty Betty's coming to see him, as well.

BABY   Oh no, not Aunty Betty. She'll have her big fat finger poking me all over. I wanna grow up!

BETTY   *(second face appears)* Oooh! Just look at the little darling! Hasn't he grown! Oh, who's Aunty Betty's little sweetie-pie, then? Coochy-coochy-cooo!

BABY   I'm not your little sweetie-pie, you old bat! You wait till I start walking. I'll crayon all over your walls! I'll stuff teddy down the toilet and flush it! Then we'll see who's a little sweetie-pie!

MUM   Would he like his bottle, then? Some nice, warm milk to fill his little tummy. Mummy get Dessy-Wessy his bottle. *(MUM's face disappears)*

BABY   Milk! Yuk! I want chocolate . . . and Coke . . . and greasy chips . . . and pizza. I wanna grow up. Help!

BETTY   Who's got his daddy's eyes, then? And his daddy's hair?

BABY   What do you mean, you daft old bat? Dad's hardly got any hair!

BETTY   I think when he grows up he's going to look just like his daddy. And he's going to be a clever, clever, clever person like his mummy.

BABY   You call that clever, the way she talks to me? And what do you mean, look like dad? I don't want to get wrinkly and bald and have hairs growing out of my nostrils. Wait a minute . . . You don't mean I'm going to grow up to be like you lot, do you? Oh no! I DON'T WANT TO GROW UP! I DON'T WANT TO GROW UP! *(starts screaming)*

*   *   *

Sometimes, growing up looks very attractive, and we can't wait. But when you think what you might turn into, perhaps it's not such a good idea after all. Just think, you might end up like me!

And isn't it strange how grown-ups are always telling kids what to do, yet adults seem to make such a mess of things themselves. Just look at what grown-ups are doing to the world today.

How can we avoid making the same mistakes our parents' generation have made?

The wisest man who ever lived is supposed to have been King Solomon. Even he did some rather foolish things in his time, but on the whole he did a very good job of being king of Israel. Here is some advice he gave to young people.

Have a group of children read **Proverbs 3:1–8 (or –12)**. Split it into sections for different readers.

This was King Solomon's secret: **"Remember the Lord in everything you do. And he will give you success."**

How do we put his wise advice into practice? He said, **". . . in everything you do."** So whatever it is we are doing, we can send up a quick prayer: "Please, Lord, show me . . . help me . . . forgive me . . . teach me . . ." or whatever it is we need at that moment. Then we pause and think before rushing into something.

As Solomon says just a bit further on,

Using his wisdom, the Lord made the earth.

Proverbs 3:19

The God who has the wisdom and understanding to make the earth must be by far the best one to show us how to live on the earth and to care for it. If we can learn to remember him in everything we do, we are likely to grow up into people who make a much better job of things than our parents' generation has.

41
The collector
card king

Theme

A modern version of the parable of the three servants as told in Matthew 25:14–30. This is written for the World Cup, but it can be rewritten for other major competitions. Actions for the characters are obvious from the text. The fifth supporter is the one to do the swaps with. He/she needs extra items for swapping.

You will need

- two narrators and five actors in football supporter gear.
- large medium and small cardboard boxes with pictures cut from magazines stuck on the outsides; card collections, scarves, etc. — whatever you can borrow.
- copies of the script. These can be printed out from *www.77talks.co.uk*.

Sketch

NARRATOR 1   There was once a *Manchester United* fan who had the biggest collection of football gear in the country. He had mountains of collector cards, piles of programmes, books full of autographs, and wardrobes full of strips. He never missed an opportunity to add to his collection. His name was Dave, but everyone called him the Collector Card King.

NARRATOR 2   Of course, Dave wasn't going to miss out on the World Cup. It was the biggest collecting opportunity of his life. But he didn't want to miss out on things back home, either.

NARRATOR 1	Dave got three of his friends together: Stu, Debra, and Mick. He gave a great big boxful of gear to Stu. "Look after it carefully," he said. "And see what you can do while I'm away."
NARRATOR 2	He gave Debra a medium-size box with the same instructions . . . And he gave Mick a boxful of World Cup cards . . . Then he left in time for the opening match.
NARRATOR 1	Stu sorted his big box of gear and set about swapping, buying and selling. With a lot of hard work and clever deals he doubled what Dave had left him.
NARRATOR 2	Debra did the same with what she had. She also doubled her collection.
NARRATOR 1	But Mick was worried in case he lost some of Dave's prize cards. He put the box under his bed, safely buried among the smelly socks and old copies of *SHOOT* magazine.
NARRATOR 2	Weeks later, after the final, Dave came home. He called his three friends together and asked to see how they had done.
NARRATOR 1	Stu spoke first. "Look," he said. "You gave me a big box of gear and I've swapped and bought and sold — and doubled what you gave me."
NARRATOR 2	"That's awesome," said Dave. "You've shown that you've got a good head for business. I'm setting up a chain of football merchandising shops. I want you to be my managing director. We're going to be rich!"
NARRATOR 1	Next, it was Debra's turn. She showed him how much she had made.
NARRATOR 2	"That's great," said Dave. "Obviously, I can

	trust you, too. I want you to be my sales manager. Welcome to the company! We're all going to be rich!"
NARRATOR 1	Then Mick produced the box of cards. It smelled of dirty socks. "I know you're a really smart businessman," said Mick. "You expect people who work for you to get results. I was afraid if I lost any of your stuff you'd be really furious, so I hid it under the bed. Here it is."
NARRATOR 2	Dave went ballistic! "You're totally useless!" he shouted. "I gave you a chance and you blew it! People who use what they are given go up in the world. But people who don't use it lose everything. Get out! And don't come begging for a job in my shops — I wouldn't even let you sweep the floor!"

After the sketch

You might ask the children to relate the main lines of the story, to ensure they have understood it. We have found a tendency for some children to be sympathetic to "Mick", so it may be helpful to point out that in real business situations, people are expected to turn in a profit — or find themselves out of a job.

In this story people are given an opportunity and expected to make something of it. Use it or lose it! This is like the skills of players in the World Cup. They have natural ability, but managers and coaches and supporters expect them to give maximum commitment, too.

You might be surprised to learn that this was a story Jesus told. We've just brought it up to date a bit. Jesus told stories like this to teach us something about life — and about God and ourselves. What was he trying to teach us in this story? . . . That this life is a shared responsibility:

God gives us gifts, abilities, time, a planet rich in resources — our part is to make the best use of these.

For those who do make good use of them, there are rich rewards. Those who don't can't expect much sympathy.

42
The biggest explosion in history

Theme

Trusting God in the most frightening circumstances.

You will need

- a Bible: Psalm 46.
- possibly pictures of volcanoes erupting — see
  www.77talks.co.uk.

Presentation

In 1628 BC there occurred the biggest explosion ever
witnessed by human beings. The noise of that explosion
was so loud that it echoed right round the world 16 times
and made people deaf 500 kilometres (300 miles) away. It
was a volcanic eruption. It was so fierce that it blew the
greater part of a Mediterranean island away.

The island was Thera, north of Crete, south-east of Greece.
Archaeologists today have discovered a mile-wide city on
one of the parts of Thera that remains. By any standards, it
was highly civilized — they even had showers and flush
toilets. They were so advanced that some people think that
there could have been TV by the time of Christ if their
civilization had continued.

But in 1628 BC a volcano on the island started erupting.
Clouds of dust and ash rained down on the town, totally
burying it — but also protecting it for future generations to
find. Then the mountain blew up. 80 cubic kilometres (50
cubic miles) of rock were blasted into the air. A tidal wave
swept across the Mediterranean. In parts of the Nile delta,
the wave was as high as a four storey building. But on one

part of the Turkish coast, trapped between two arms of land like a funnel, the wave reached an incredible 250 metres (800 feet) high. It swept 50 kilometres (30 miles) inland, scouring the earth bare and leaving "scablands" that are still visible today.[1]

Seven years without summer

Fine dust flung high into the atmosphere blocked out the sun and turned the following summer into winter. 5,000-year-old bristlecone pines in California bear the scars of the summer frosts on their growth rings for that year. Chinese records show that all the crops died and that the effects continued for seven years. Great numbers of people died of starvation in northern China, and that must have been true around the world.

Psalm 46 in the Bible may be a memory of that cataclysmic event.

Read the whole psalm, or selected verses from it.

Something to think about

This ancient song shows the writer's confidence in God in the most frightening circumstances. Many people know the first sentence by heart: **"God is our refuge and strength, an ever-present help in trouble."** If someone could write that, after living through the biggest explosion in human history, then that is worth listening to. We shall all face disasters, either great or small. We shall all be in frightening situations. The sort of confidence that can trust God in the worst possible situations must be worth having. **"God is our refuge and strength, an ever-present help in trouble."**

NOTE

1 Details about Thera from *Return to Sodom and Gomorrah,* Charles Pellegrino (TSP, 1994), chapter 9.

43
Ways to praise

Theme

There are many ways and reasons to praise God — and they are all good for you.

You will need

- sports gear associated with a local or popular sports team, e.g. scarves, rattles.
- a book, a video, art reproduction etc., as below.

Presentation

Talk about — or, better, get some fans to talk about — a favourite team and demonstrate how supporters react when the team wins.

That is one of the ways people behave when they think something or someone is really great.

Lots of us are fans of other things besides sports. How do we show we think something is great in these following cases?

Music or theatre performance — we applaud.

A book or a film or a song — we tell others how good it is and encourage them to read or see or buy it.

A work of art — we gaze at it, take it in, see new things in it.

A hero or an expert in a field we are interested in — we try to copy them, learn from them, be like them.

These are all different ways of praising people we appreciate. The bigger the group we are in, the noisier we tend to be in our appreciation and the more we can let our hair down. But no one way is really any better than another.

Applaud a robin

If people are worth praising because of their skill or their creativity, how much more is God, the Creator of everything! . . . We don't normally scream and shout when we see a beautiful sunset, or applaud a robin singing, but we may pause to appreciate them.

The Bible is full of ways people have praised God, the book of Psalms especially.

In **Psalm 150** people praise God with loud music and dancing, much like fans at a football match.

In **Psalm 8** David praises God as he gazes at the stars and thinks about what it means to be a human being in the universe God has created.

Psalm 119 is full of praise for God's guidelines for living. The writer shows his appreciation by wanting to put them into practice and follow the guidelines.

The writer of **Psalm 78** sees the great things God has done and wants to tell everyone about them.

So the way we praise depends on the kind of person we are, the sort of things we appreciate most, and whether we are alone or with a group of other people. But however we praise, it makes us feel good. And it makes us feel closer to the person we are praising; it creates a relationship between us. Praising God draws us closer to him and leaves us with a warm, peaceful feeling.

So if we want to make our day better — any day — let's try praising God. We can praise him for things we see in the natural world, people we appreciate, things he has done. We can praise silently or in words or song. We can praise by telling other people something or by putting into action something we have learned in the Bible. Try it. It does you good!

Something to do

Put praise into practice with a noisy song or with quiet appreciation of a piece of music.

44
Here's mud in your eye!

Theme

A mouth-watering introduction leads into the story of Jesus healing a blind man in John 9:1–11 and the conclusion that God treats us all as individuals.

You will need

- possibly something good to eat; a 1.5 litre soft drink bottle.
- You could use the cartoon from the *www.77talks.co.uk* website.

Presentation

Lovingly describe a meal that should appeal to your group, or eat something appetizing in front of them. Ask whose mouth is watering.

We make saliva — or spit — all the time, but especially when we start to think about food. Would anybody like to guess how much we produce in a day? A cupful? . . . Half a litre? . . . In fact, the average person produces 1.5 litres (2.5 pints) of saliva every day — enough to fill a large cola bottle. That is nothing compared to cows. [Show the cartoon if you have it.] A cow makes over 50 litres (85 pints) of spit a day!

Saliva is vital to turning the solid food we put into our mouths into a moist paste that we can swallow, but it also starts the digestive process. It has other uses as well. If you hurt your finger or get a splinter in it, what do you instinctively do? . . . Put it in your mouth and suck it. And if you fall over while you are out, you are likely to rub spit on the graze.

As so often, what we do instinctively is a good thing to do. Saliva is a natural antiseptic. Researchers at St Bartholomew's hospital in London got volunteers to lick their hands. They found that this produced a powerful microbe killer [nitric oxide]. We all carry around a useful emergency first-aid kit in our mouths!

It sounds strange, but Jesus once used spit when he healed a blind man. **Tell the story found in John 9:1–11.**

Another time, Jesus healed a blind man with just a word. Why did he use mud made with saliva this time? Was it because saliva is a good antiseptic, or was there another reason?

Nobody knows the answer to that. Perhaps this man needed something physical to happen to help him believe. When we look at the various stories of Jesus healing people, we find that they are all different. Sometimes he touched the person, sometimes he didn't. Sometimes he told them to do something, either before or after they were healed. What we can see is that he treated each one as an individual. He knew what would be helpful to each person.

A prayer

Father God, we thank you for the first-aid antiseptic in our saliva that is always there, ready to use at a moment's notice. But we thank you more for the way you know each one of us personally and know just what we need. Help us to turn to you when we are in need and to trust you to heal our deepest hurts. Amen.

Right for Me,
Right for the World

Changing the world begins
with changing our own hearts

45
Heart to change the world

Theme

Cleaning up the mess inside us is just as important as cleaning up the world.

You will need

• Make a giant heart as follows. Get a sheet of thick card, e.g. the side of a box. Fold a sheet of paper the same size in half; draw half a heart on it; cut out, open out, and trace onto the card. Cut out and paint red (auto spray paint is perfect for this). Glue a box, e.g. a cereal packet, to the back. On a discarded soft drink can write "GREEDY" with a marker pen. Similarly, write "CARELESS" on, for example, a yoghurt pot, and "SELFISH" on a piece of rag. Place this "rubbish" inside the box fixed to the back of the heart.

Presentation

Do you have a heart to save the world? Every so often, politicians meet to try to agree on limiting emissions of greenhouse gasses. It is an uphill battle. There are too many people who don't want to change their lifestyle, too many who don't care what the world may be like in 50 or 100 years' time, because it doesn't affect them now.

Centuries ago, God gave the prophet Jeremiah a terrifying vision of a ruined world. This is what he saw:

> I looked at the earth. It was empty and had no shape! I looked at the sky. And its light was gone. I looked at the mountains, and they were shaking! All the hills were trembling. I looked, and there were no

people! Every bird in the sky had flown away. I looked, and the good, rich land had become a desert! All its towns had been destroyed. The Lord and his great anger has caused this. *Jeremiah 4:23–26*

Although the situation was a different one then, the causes and results seem very similar. God said to the people, "**The way you have lived and acted has brought this trouble to you.**" (Jeremiah 4:18) If global warming causes rising sea-levels and many other disasters, it will be because of the way we have lived and acted.

Do you have a heart to save the world? It's a big job; it needs a big heart.

[Produce your giant heart.]

Many children and young people obviously do have a heart to save the world. We can see that in things like recycling schemes. (Refer to anything you know the children are involved in.) But before we get too smug, we ought to look at our hearts very carefully.

[Ask for a volunteer to look inside the heart and pull out a piece of what he or she finds there.]

When we look at this heart, we find there's some rubbish inside. This cola can, what does it have written on it? . . . "GREEDY". Let's be honest — hands up — who is greedy sometimes? . . . All of us? Yes. Can any of us honestly say we weren't greedy in what we wanted for Christmas?

[A second volunteer takes out a piece of rubbish.]

What does this say? . . . "CARELESS". Hands up, who is careless sometimes? . . . Who throws a bit of litter down occasionally? . . . Who forgets to turn lights off, or leaves doors open in winter? . . . All of us.

[Third volunteer takes out the last piece of rubbish.]

What does this say? . . . "SELFISH". Who's selfish sometimes? . . . "Me first!" "It's all mine!" "I don't want to share!" . . .

A clean heart

Greedy, careless, selfish — when we are honest we know that we've all got some of that kind of rubbish inside us. Just before that terrible vision of a ruined world, God said this through Jeremiah,

> **People of Jerusalem, clean the evil from your hearts and be saved.**
> *Jeremiah 4:14*

The message is the same now as it was around 2,600 years ago. If you've got a heart to save the world, it has to be a clean heart. It's no good trying to clean up the problems out there if there is a mess inside. Sooner or later the rubbish inside starts to cause trouble, no matter how good our intentions are. To save the world will need some big changes in lifestyle for each one of us. Some of us may be surprised to find how greedy or selfish we really are when it comes to making those changes.

One of the lines in the Lord's Prayer is, "Forgive us our trespasses" or "Forgive us the wrongs we have done". That is really asking God to do a clean-up job on our hearts, to get rid of the rubbish there. So perhaps we might pray something like this:

A prayer

Our Father in heaven, we have all put up our hands to confess that sometimes we are greedy, selfish and careless. Forgive us the wrong things we have done. Clean us up inside. And give us a big heart, a heart to save the world. Amen.

46
Yoghurt race

Theme

Wrong thinking leads to trouble.

You will need

- runny (not "set") fruit yoghurts, preferably well coloured; two or three bowls and spoons; cloths to clean up with; carpet offcuts or cloth pads to go under people's heads; stable, flat-seated chairs.
- If the group is large, this needs to be done on a platform for visibility.

Presentation

Ask for two or three tough volunteers for a yoghurt-eating race. Get each one to lie stomach-down across a chair with his head resting on the floor and his left hand behind his back (or right hand if left-handed). Place a bowl of yoghurt and spoon in front of each one's face. On the signal, they simply have to eat the yoghurt as fast as possible. First one to finish wins.

When finished, get them to stand up so the group can see their faces before they clean up. What a mess!

Maybe part of the reason the world is in a mess is because people try to do things while their *thinking* is all upside down.

Money is one example. There is nothing wrong with money, or earning it, or spending it. But when people put it *first,* it stops being a useful tool and leads them into all kinds of wrong. As Paul said in the Bible:

The love of money causes all kinds of evil. Some people have left the true faith because they want to get more and more money. But they have caused themselves a great deal of sorrow. *1 Timothy 6:10*

Paul is talking there about the mess that can come from upside-down thinking about money.

Another example is freedom. As human beings, we are free to think, free to make choices, free to explore. It is one of the greatest privileges we have. But it is very easy to get our thinking about freedom upside-down and use it in the wrong way. That way lies disaster. Listen to Paul again:

My brothers. God called you to be free. But do not use your freedom as an excuse to do the things that please your sinful self . . . If you go on hurting each other and tearing each other apart, be careful! You will completely destroy each other.
Galatians 5:13, 15

A real-life example from your own experience of getting into a mess through misusing your freedom would be helpful here.

Hold up the towel that has been used to clean up someone's face. The great message of the Bible is that when we do get into a mess, God is always waiting to clean us up when we turn to him for help.

A prayer

Father God, please show us how to sort out our thinking *before* we get into a mess. But when we do do something stupid, help us to recognize our fault and say sorry. Remind us that you are always there, always ready with a towel to clean us up and turn our lives the right way up. Amen.

47
The cost of water

Theme

The importance of thinking about the real costs of what we do and say.

You will need

- a bottle of mineral water and a jug of tap water.
- The Bible story is found in 1 Chronicles 11:15–19.

Presentation

[Hold up the jug of water.] We each use nearly 4.5 litres of water a day for drinking and cooking. (Of course, we use much more for things like flushing the toilet and washing clothes.) Most of this water comes through pipes into our homes and all we have to do is turn on the tap and it flows out freely. But over the past few years, more and more people have started buying bottled water to drink. This is probably partly due to advertising and partly to people taking holidays in countries where it is more normal to drink bottled water, or necessary because of poor water quality.

If we are concerned about the environment, which one of these should we drink? Is it better to drink tap water or bottled water? . . . How did the bottled water get to the supermarket? . . . By lorry. It added to the congestion on the roads, used diesel, added to carbon dioxide emissions and pollution. Then there are the materials and energy used to make the bottle, and after use, the bottle is more waste to be disposed of or, perhaps, recycled. The cost of tap water to the environment is tiny by comparison.

Water from Bethlehem

In the Old Testament there is a story about David — the one who killed Goliath — and a drink of water. After David became king of Israel, there was a war with the Philistines. The Philistines had taken Bethlehem — which was David's home town — and had a garrison of soldiers there.

David and his men were camped by a cave in the wilderness. It was a hot and dusty place. David had a real craving for some water from the well by the gate at Bethlehem, the well he had drunk from so often as a child. Some of his men overheard him, and three of them decided on a madcap mission. They broke through the enemy lines, drew some water from the well at Bethlehem and carried it back to David.

You might think that he would have been delighted. Not at all. He refused to drink it and poured it on the ground instead. Why? It seems very ungrateful! But David knew what the real cost of that water was. His men might have been captured and killed. The lives of his friends were far more valuable to him than enjoying a drink of fresh water. He was not prepared for his men to risk their lives for his pleasure. The cost was far too great.

Something to think about

The cost to the environment of a bottle of water is far greater than the cost of a jug of tap water. (It costs a lot more money, too!) Perhaps we should think about refusing to drink it, like David, because of the cost. It is only a small thing, but it is one of the many small things people need to think about in order to look after God's world properly.

48
Reactions and rewards

Theme

One of the moral laws of the universe: we reap what we sow.

You will need

- a ball to bounce.
- possibly a bicycle.

Presentation

Come in bouncing a ball — save the reason for later. Ask for an athletic and fearless volunteer. The volunteer's mission — should they choose to accept it — is to put their head down and run as fast as they can into the side or back wall of the hall without stopping. Will they do it? Of course not! (But be prepared to stop the suicidal nutter who says yes!)

Why not? Because they know Newton's law of action and reaction. Don't they? . . . Well, perhaps not in words, but everyone knows it from experience. Sir Isaac Newton was one of the greatest scientists who ever lived. Newton's third law says that for every action, there is an equal and opposite reaction. In other words, if you hit the wall with your head, the wall hits you back equally hard. That's why it hurts. The good bit about this is that if you throw a ball on the floor, the floor obligingly hits it back to you. It's nice to have a floor that plays ball, isn't it? (Thank your hard-headed — or level-headed — volunteer and let him or her sit down.)

This law is one of the fundamental laws of the universe. Babies learn it the first time they bump their head against the table, but it takes a genius like Sir Isaac Newton to

174

think it through and put it into words — or rather, into mathematics. Knowing the law stops us from riding our bicycles into the front of a bus.

Road pushes cyclist

The law also enables the bike to work in the first place. You push on the pedal which moves the chain which turns the wheel which pushes against the road — and the road pushes back equally hard and sends you a few metres nearer the chip shop or the winning tape of the Tour de France.

Is there a similar law for the way people behave? If you punch someone in the playground will they punch you back equally hard? Not necessarily. They might punch you harder! Or they might not retaliate at all. Quite often, we do not seem to get any punishment for a bad action. We do something and "get away with it". Equally, quite often we do not get any reward for a good action. Nobody notices the good thing we have done.

Or so it seems.

There is a famous thing that Jesus said about doing good. In this case, the good action he talked about was helping those in need. He said,

> **When you give to the poor, don't let anyone know what you are doing. Your giving should be done in secret. Your Father [God] can see what is done in secret and he will reward you.** *Matthew 6:3–4*

That reward isn't like Newton's "equal and opposite reaction". When you throw the ball on the floor, you don't have to wait ten minutes for the floor to decide to bounce it back to you. (Just think what a game of tennis would be like if you did!) God's rewards usually involve waiting. But what Jesus gives us here is a promise that the reward will

175

come — in God's time. If we are quietly generous, God will be generous to us when the time is right.

Planting selfishness

Does that also apply to bad or hurtful things we do? St Paul said it did, in one of his letters in the Bible. He uses a different picture, the picture of sowing seeds and waiting for the crop to grow. That gives a clearer idea of the time involved. He wrote,

> **Don't be misled: No one makes a fool of God. What a person plants, he will harvest. The person who plants selfishness, ignoring the needs of others — ignoring God! — harvests a crop of weeds. All he will have to show for his life is weeds!**
>
> *Galatians 6:7–8*, The Message

[Bounce the ball again.]

If you throw a ball against a wall, the wall bounces the ball back to you. If we do something hurtful or selfish, that will eventually bounce back on us as well — unless we say sorry and ask for forgiveness. But if we are generous and do good to others without making a fuss about it, God who sees everything will reward us for it. That's what Jesus promised.

Something to think about

Paul went on to say:

> **The one who plants in response to God, letting God's Spirit do the growth work in him, harvests a crop of real life, eternal life.**

Let's have a few moments of quiet. We can ask God's Spirit to show us something generous, something kind, something helpful that we could do quietly today.

49
Animal welfare

Theme

Our responsibility to take care of God's creation.

You will need

- three children to read the Bible verses.
- recent examples of cruelty to animals — check the RSPCA website: *www.rspca.org.uk.*

Presentation

Despite years of efforts by animal welfare campaigners, people go on being cruel to animals. (Give examples.)

The Bible teaches that this is not what God wants. He created the world, and we read in Genesis 1 that he was pleased with all he had made. Many other passages in the Bible teach us how God cares and provides for the living creatures he has made. Here are some extracts from **Psalm 104**:

READER A "You make springs pour into the ravines; they flow between the mountains. They water all the wild animals; the wild donkeys come there to drink. Wild birds make nests by the water; they sing among the branches." (verses 10–12)

READER B "You make the grass grow for cattle, and vegetables for the people. You make food grow from the earth." (verse 14)

READER C "The lions roar for their prey and seek their food from God . . . These all look to you to give them their food at the proper time. When you give it to them, they gather it up;

when you open your hand, they are satisfied
with good things." (verses 21, 27–28)

That is God's part in creation, but looking after animals is
our responsibility, too. Here are some guidelines which,
although they were written two to three thousand years
ago, are still helpful principles today:

READER A   "Good people take care of their animals."
                 (Proverbs 12:10)
READER B   "If you happen to see your enemy's cow or
                 donkey running loose, take it back to him. If
                 his donkey has fallen under its load, help him
                 get the donkey to its feet again; don't just
                 walk off." (Exodus 23:4–5)

Some of the stories Jesus told, and the things he said, echo
these important principles and reinforce the need for us to
treat animals humanely. In fact, in John 10:14–15 Jesus
says, **"I am the Good Shepherd who lays his life down
for his sheep."** In this picture, Jesus says that because the
shepherd cares so much for his sheep, he is even prepared
to risk his life by defending them against wolves. As well as
teaching us about God's love and protection for us, this
gives us a perfect example of how Jesus wants us to care for
those around us, animals as well as people.

The Bible makes it clear that God has trusted us to look
after everything he has created. If we let him down, we are
the ones who will have to answer to him. Relying on
someone else to look after our world simply isn't good
enough. If we sit back and watch while others destroy it,
then we are as guilty as they are for spoiling it.

Whether we are talking about local traffic pollution, the
treatment of animals in zoos, the felling of tropical
rainforests, global warming, or Third World poverty, God
has given us all a duty to stand up for what is right. Before
it's too late.

50
Stop children

Theme

God's big STOP signs — the Ten Commandments — are there for our protection.

You will need

- to borrow a road-crossing "lollipop" and clothing from your local friendly school-crossing person.
- pictures of other road signs (e.g. printed out from a clip-art collection or at *www.77talks.co.uk*) and a copy of the *Highway Code*.

Presentation

Show the "lollipop". It says, "STOP CHILDREN". Stop children what? Stop children using their mobile phones in class? Stop children watching too much TV? Stop children pestering adults? Or what?

Elicit from the children what the sign means: Stop . . . because there are children waiting to cross the road. Stop . . . to prevent an accident. Stop . . . to save someone from getting hurt.

In other words, it is not a sign to prevent us from doing something we like doing. It is a sign for our protection. How many children have been saved from being killed or seriously injured because of the lollipop woman or man on the way to school?

To develop this further, other road signs can be shown and the children asked what they mean. A sign like "Beware of the frogs" can cause a lot of amusement. There really is one! Give one child a copy of the *Highway Code* and see if he or she can find it. Emphasize that these signs are for our protection.

Get another child to come and hold up a Bible. God has a number of STOP signs, too. Things like: Stop telling lies about other people. Stop stealing. Stop using God's name as a swear word. Stop working seven days a week — take a day off to appreciate God's work in making this wonderful world.

There are ten big STOP signs like these in the Bible. Who knows what we call them? . . . Get the child with the Bible to find Exodus 20 and read the heading: The Ten Commandments. (Most Bibles have a heading like this. Check in advance.)

Parents are old fuddy-duddies?

God's other big STOP signs are: Stop making anything other than me a "god" in your life. Stop worshipping anything that is merely made by human beings. Stop thinking that your parents are old fuddy-duddies who know nothing. Stop committing murder. Stop being unfaithful to the person you marry. Stop wanting what belongs to other people.

What are the STOP lollipop and the signs in the *Highway Code* for? . . . For our protection. To save lives. To stop children being injured. So what do you think God's big STOP signs are for? . . . Just the same. To protect us. To stop us getting hurt. Even to save our lives.

Some people don't think that road signs apply to them. They drive through red traffic lights. They ignore warning signs. They drive too fast.

Some people don't think the Ten Commandments apply to them. They ignore God's STOP signs and nothing seems to happen. But sooner or later, there's a crash. People get hurt. And it's often not just the one who ignored the signs who gets hurt. Others do, too.

So a big "Thank you" to the crossing lady who keeps us safe on the journey to school. And an even bigger "Thanks" to the one who made ten giant lollipop signs to keep us safe on our journey through life.

Something to do

Make a series of lollipop STOP signs and write the Ten Commandments on them.

NOTE

The authors wish to pay their respects to the woman in Barnsley who pointed out to a friend that the town council had provided a lollipop man on Sunday — when it was double-time, too. How kind of the council!

51
Tramp takes all

Theme

God gave us seven days in a week and asked us to keep one specially for him.

You will need

- to dress up as a tramp or a bag-lady. The more realistic you look the more effective the talk will be.

Presentation

Be found curled up asleep when the meeting or service starts and don't be disturbed by people coming in. When the leader or minister (who is, of course, in the know) gets to the talk, you interrupt and say you will do the talking today. You make it quite clear that you are capable of doing a far better job than the one at the front!

(On one occasion during a church service, a woman went to fetch the police and had to be persuaded to desist by a well-known member of the congregation. Be prepared!)

Tell this story:

An old tramp visited a family, and the woman of the house took pity on him. She gave him something to eat, and then decided she would go further than that, and allowed him to have a bath. She agreed with him that he would throw away his old clothes — she found some of her husband's clothes, and fitted him up with a totally new outfit. He was very grateful. Then she decided that as he left, she would make him a flask of coffee and some sandwiches to help him on his way. He was even more grateful.

The tramp was so well mannered and so full of thanks that the woman was moved to do even more for him. "Now," she said, "I have a box here, and in it there are seven gold coins that my father gave to me. They have lain for many years doing nothing in this box. I am going to give you six of them, but I want to keep one of them for myself." The tramp was even more grateful and thanked her over and over again. Then he went on his way.

All in a good cause

When her husband came home later, she told him that some of his clothes had been given to an old tramp, including his best gardening jacket, and a decent pair of boots. He frowned at first, but then said he supposed it was all in a good cause. They went to bed.

In the middle of the night, there was a noise and the woman said to her husband, "I think there's someone downstairs." He just grunted and turned over to go back to sleep, but then they both heard a bump. He got his cricket bat out of the wardrobe and crept downstairs. He peeked through the crack in the door.

Guess who it was?

[The children will all rush to tell you it was the tramp.] What do you think he was doing? . . . He was stealing that gold coin, the last one left in the box. What do you think of him and what he did? . . .

Of course, we would never do anything like that! . . . Would we?

God gave us seven days of the week and asked us to keep one specially for him. He said it was a day to rest from working, a holy day, a day to remember him and to give him honour. But people actually steal it and won't recognize the one who gave it. We are all so busy that we think we don't have time to take a day off from shopping, we don't have time to take a day off from getting jobs done, we don't have time to take a day to relax and come close to God.

Who is really the loser, God or us?

A prayer

Father God, you rested after you had made the world. You told us to rest on the seventh day, too. Help us to realize how foolish we are when we try to steal that day and use it to go on being busy. Help us to discover how much richer we are when we take time to come close to you. Amen.

Beyond Cyberspace

The ultimate in communication is as close as a whispered prayer or a summer daydream

'OK, vere is ze patient?'

52
Mobile phone 1

Theme

We should keep on praying for justice, knowing that God will answer.

You will need

- a mobile phone; a story that you can start reading or telling that gets interrupted.
- an assistant with a phone and your number, set for quick-dial. This assistant should be right at the back or in an adjoining room and have the phone hidden.

Presentation

Start telling a story. When you have been going for half a minute or so, your assistant presses their quick-dial button to call you. You look round the group to see whose phone is ringing, realize it is yours, apologize, and answer it. You hold a quick conversation (imagining the other side so that your assistant does not have to speak and reveal himself), telling the other person where you are and that you can't help them just now.

Apologize again and continue with the story. The same thing happens a couple more times, and each time you get more forthright with the imaginary caller.

The final time it rings, you sigh in resignation and give the caller the information they want. (This could be an imaginary name, address and phone number or — for a laugh at your own expense — some information connected to what people know is an interest of yours.)

Now abandon your original story and tell a different one instead — the story of the persistent widow from **Luke 18:1–8**.

Underline the point that the judge in the story was a bad judge. If even a bad judge gave the woman justice because of her persistence, how much more will God answer prayers for justice! We may not see those answers immediately, but God's heart is for justice on earth, and we can be sure those prayers will receive an answer. Just keep dialling God's number!

Prayers

A group of children could be asked in advance to prepare some prayers on a justice issue.

53
Mobile phone 2

Theme

A practical and fun lesson in praying for people and blessing them.

You will need

- a mobile phone.
- Do some detective work in advance and find a couple of relevant phone numbers in case the group can't come up with any themselves.

Presentation

In a school assembly, for example, talk to the children and find out whose mum is at home and may be feeling a bit down or unwell. In a church situation, it is more likely to be a grandparent who is at home, perhaps alone.

Suggest that a phone call might cheer them up, and get out your mobile. Children will usually know their home number, so that is easy. In church, for a grandparent, often the parent is present and will know or have the number.

When you get through, chat to the person as though you know them. Then say that there are lots of people who want to say hello, and get all the children to shout, "Hello, Mrs Jones!" Then pass the phone to the child/grandchild for a quick word.

A big amen

As this is church/worship, say you would like to pray for the person. Ask if you may (very few people refuse when one offers to pray for them), and if there is anything particular she would like prayer for. Then pray a simple prayer — with a big "Amen!" at the end from everyone with you.

This can be repeated two or three times. For subsequent calls, one of the children might offer to say the prayer.

Just doing this is such a strong and memorable lesson in itself that it doesn't really need anything added. If you wish, underline the point that praying is a natural thing that anyone can do anywhere and at any time. It always blesses people.

NOTE

One of the authors used this in a different way and spoke to a father who was at home on a Sunday morning, doing odd jobs. Following a big "Hello" from the congregation and a word with the daughter, he asked him where he ought to be. "Well, at church, really." The father promised to come to church that evening, the author was invited to the home for tea, the man was converted — and is now a Methodist lay preacher!

54
Mobile phone 3

Theme

People pray in different ways. The important thing is keeping in contact with God, not how you do it.

You will need

- a mobile phone; a fixed-line phone (unplugged).

Presentation

Ask some of the children what they like doing with friends. Playing will come out high on the list, but just chatting is usually close behind. Telling good news or sharing things that worry them are important things, too.

That's really what prayer is: talking to God, telling him about things that excite you, sharing worries and fears.

There are different ways of praying. For some people, the way they prefer is like this. [Produce the fixed-line phone.] This kind of phone stays in one place. If you want to talk to someone on it, you need to go to the phone. That means you can't use it when you are out and about. Some people pray mainly like this, at a particular time or in a particular place. It may be that they put aside some time to spend with God first thing in the morning or last thing at night. It may be that they find the best place to pray is in church or in a special quiet place at home. Perhaps they light a candle or use some prayers from a book.

Always close

Others prefer to pray like this. [Produce the mobile phone.] They like to talk to God any time, any place. They may pray while they are on the move or doing other things. They find it very helpful to know that God is always around, always close, and that you can chat to him, just like a best friend.

One way of praying isn't better than another. It partly depends on the kind of person you are, and what you have learned from the example of other people or, if you go to church, the kind of church it is.

When Paul wrote to the church in Thessalonica, in Greece, he said:

> **Always be happy. Never stop praying. Give thanks whatever happens. This is what God wants for you in Christ Jesus.** *1 Thessalonians 5:16–18*

So put a smile on your face. Look around at all the things there are to be thankful for. And get on the phone to God!

55
The miracle well

Theme

Answer to prayer can seem a long time coming, but when it does, God's generosity can surprise us.

You will need

- A copy of the photo at *www.77talks.co.uk* printed onto an overhead transparency will help bring the story alive. It shows water gushing from the borehole.

Presentation

In the south of France, in an old farmhouse perched on a mountain ridge, live an English couple, Tony and Georgina Clay, and their two children. Georgina is a district nurse who drives around the local villages caring for people in their homes. Tony looks after vines, renovates the house and writes songs — he used to have a band that toured schools in England.

Just north of their house is a mountainside that drops some 250 metres (800 feet) to the valley below. To the south, they look across valleys and ridges to the snow-capped peak of Mount Canigou in the Pyrenees. It is a beautiful spot to live in, but the nearest village is two kilometres away, the nearest shop is three kilometres down the mountainside, and they have no water or electricity!

When they bought the house in 1994 there was a small spring about 50 metres from the house for water, but it was only a trickle and it soon dried up. While Georgie collected drinking water on her rounds, from one of the village fountains, Tony fixed guttering and rigged up tanks and pipes and pumps to try to supply rainwater for washing and flushing the toilet. But there was never enough. To make matters worse, there has been less rainfall in recent years in the region, and even some whole villages are running out of water.

Praying for a solution

Tony and Georgie loved the place and believed God wanted them there. There are very few Christians in the area and most people never give God a thought. As Georgie cared for the sick and elderly in the region, and as Tony demonstrated honesty and being a good neighbour, they were quietly showing God's love. They kept praying for a solution to the water problem, but it seemed to get worse, not better.

There is a bit in the book of Isaiah that talks about a person who does and says what is right. It goes on,

> ... this is the man who will dwell on the heights, whose refuge will be the mountain fortress. His bread will be supplied, and water will not fail him.
>
> *Isaiah 33:16*, New International Version

That sounds like a good promise, but it gets hard to believe when you keep praying and nothing happens. At times things got really desperate, for example, when Tony fell off a horse and broke three ribs in his back. He was in severe pain for several months. It was winter and it was almost impossible for him to fetch water, start the electricity generator, or cut wood for the fire.

The only solution seemed to be to hire a company to drill a borehole. That is quite common in rural France, but it is very expensive. You have to pay for every metre that is drilled and there is no guarantee that you will hit water, especially living on a mountain ridge. And there is no technology that can tell you the right place to drill.

In 2000, with horses to water as well as their own needs, they decided to go for a borehole. They took the best advice they could get and started the drilling close to the house, only a few metres from the mountainside to the north. It was a Tuesday not long before Christmas. Tony asked the company to go down 35 metres (115 feet). By the end of the day, they had found just a trickle of water. What now? If they stopped they would waste the money they had spent so far. If they went on drilling, there was still no guarantee of finding water and they could waste even more money. What would *you* have done?

Sleepless night

Tony and Georgie prayed, and got on the phone to ask friends to pray, too. Tony had a sleepless night. In the morning he had taken a decision. He told the drilling company to continue down to 45 metres (145 feet).

At 45 metres, nothing. But as the drill was in two-metre (six-foot) lengths, they went another metre for good measure — and the drill hit soft mud. A little bit deeper and water started rising up the borehole.

Was that an answer to prayer — or was it just coincidence?

That evening the engineers tested the flow of water. It was 6000 litres (1270 gallons) — six tonnes — of water per hour! The drilling company had never hit such a flow of water at such a height. They were 250 metres (800 feet) above the valley floor, but they seemed to have hit an underground river. The water must have been coming from many miles away. What a Christmas present!

Tony and Georgie now have enough water for themselves, the horses, a guest house when Tony has finished converting the barn — even a swimming pool. ". . . **This is the man who will dwell on the heights, whose refuge**

will be the mountain fortress. His bread will be
supplied and water will not fail him."

Something to think about

Jesus told stories to encourage people to go on praying
even when it feels like God isn't listening. Tony and
Georgie had six years of struggling and praying when it
seemed like God wasn't listening. At times they were
tempted to give up. If you feel like that sometimes, turn
your tap on and remember the miracle well.

56
Arresting prayer

Theme

**Why isn't prayer always answered in the way we would like?
A true story suggests one answer.**

You will need

• Nothing needed.

Presentation

What happens if you pray and your prayer doesn't get
answered? Do you think it's a waste of time and give up?
Here is a true story about the head-teacher of a school and
what happened when she prayed.

It was a fortnight into the summer holidays when Mrs
Hammond[1] got a phone call from the school caretaker.
Twenty-three windows at the back of the school had been
broken. Mrs Hammond went to see and thought about
how much it was going to cost to replace them.

She was also worried that whoever did it would come back
and break into the school and do more damage inside.

Mrs Hammond has had lots of experience of God
answering prayer, so she rang up two of her friends and
asked them to come with her to the school the next
evening and ask God to protect it. At the same time, Mrs
Hammond took some letters to a house over the road. The
letters asked people to keep an eye on the school and to
phone for the police if they saw anyone inside the
grounds. Some of the children were going to deliver the
letters to all the houses near the school.

Love your enemies

Then the three of them walked round the grass at the back and saw the place in the fence where people had probably climbed over. Mrs Hammond was fairly sure that it was some children who had broken the windows. They prayed, asking God to protect the school from more damage. They remembered that Jesus said that we should love our enemies and pray for those who hurt us **(Matthew 5:44)**, so they asked God to bless the people who had broken the windows. They must be very unhappy people if the best they could think of to do in the summer holidays was to go round breaking school windows!

A week later, the phone rang again. Seventeen of the windows that had been mended had been broken again! Now Mrs Hammond was even more worried. The caretaker was on holiday and she was going on holiday herself the very next day. She had prayed for the school to be protected against more damage, and now there were 17 more windows to be paid for!

A waste of time?

What would most of us have thought at that moment? Probably, that praying had been a waste of time. Maybe God isn't interested in school windows, or maybe he had more important things to do. But Mrs Hammond didn't think that like. She knew the bit in the Bible where Jesus says to go on praying and not stop. She went back to the school, and this time she took her husband with her.

They asked God to protect the school again, but Mr Hammond prayed a different prayer. He prayed that whoever was breaking the windows would be caught.

Then they went off, leaving the main gate unlocked because the gardeners were coming to work in the grounds that day. That meant they had to go back at the end of the afternoon to lock the gate again after the gardeners had finished. When they arrived, some of the children in the street asked if they could go round the back and see the broken windows. Mrs Hammond wasn't very keen, but these were children who were helping keep an eye on the school, so she said yes. They went round the back while Mr and Mrs Hammond went inside the school.

We've caught them!

Suddenly, there was lots of shouting. "Mrs Hammond! Mrs Hammond! We've caught them! We've caught them!" Mr and Mrs Hammond ran round to the back of the school. Sure enough, the children had caught two boys. One of them had even got into the school through a broken window. They were two boys who had been at the school when they were younger. They confessed that it was them who had broken the windows. The police were called and came and took the boys away.

So what about the first prayer? Why wasn't that answered? Well, maybe it was. Maybe God knew that the best way to bless those boys was for them to get caught. Perhaps getting caught will stop them from doing something more serious later and getting into bigger trouble. Only God knows. That is one reason why, when we pray and don't seem to get an answer, we should not give up. God knows what is best. If we trust him and leave the way he answers prayer up to him, sooner or later we shall see some exciting answers.

NOTE

1 Name altered.

57
Volcanoes and earthquakes

Theme

Children rightly ask how a good God could allow volcanoes and earthquakes, with all the destruction and loss of life they cause. A part of the answer is that life on earth would be impossible without them.

You will need

- pictures of volcanoes or destruction caused by earthquakes, from reference books or from links at *www.77talks.co.uk.*
- a piece of chalk.

Presentation

Begin by referring to any recent news item, or discussing with children what they have seen on films or in books.

Many of us enjoy seeing the spectacular pictures of volcanoes, but when we hear about disasters in which towns get destroyed and people killed, we are bound to ask questions. "Why does God allow earthquakes?" "Why do people get killed when volcanoes erupt?"

Like all the questions about death and suffering, there are no simple answers. One of the things we do now know is that without earthquakes and volcanoes we would not even be alive to ask the questions. Here is why.

Who knows about greenhouse gases? . . . These are gases in the atmosphere that trap heat from the sun. At the present time, scientists are almost certain that the greenhouse effect is actually happening. A build-up of these gases in the atmosphere is leading to the earth warming up. Which is the gas which is the biggest cause of the problem? Breathe out! . . . Carbon dioxide, a gas we all pump into the atmosphere every time we breathe. Burning fossil fuels such as natural gas and petrol produces far more.

The freezer effect

So we all know about the greenhouse effect and some of its possible dangers. But the effect also works in reverse. What would happen if the amount of carbon dioxide in the air decreased? . . . Yes, the earth would get colder. Some people call that "the freezer effect". Planet earth would become an ice-planet. No liquid seas, no rain . . . no life! No *you* and *me*!

Why should the amount of carbon dioxide in the atmosphere decrease? Well, it's happening all the time. Water in clouds, and carbon dioxide in the air, react together. They make a weak acid. When that acid falls as rain, it reacts with rock, and the carbon dioxide gets locked into solids known as carbonates. Here is an example. [Show a piece of chalk.] This is calcium carbonate. For example, the North and South Downs in the south of England are hills made of chalk. Where they meet the sea they are cut off, forming the famous white cliffs of Dover.

Millions of years of that happening and we would not even have been here to be worrying about the greenhouse effect! All the carbon dioxide would have been locked up in the earth's rocks. But something happens on earth that doesn't happen on a planet like Mars.

The earth's surface is made of vast plates that are slowly but surely moving, carrying the continents with them. When the edge of one plate rides up over another, mountains are formed. When one plate slides past another, it causes shocks — earthquakes. And when parts of plates carrying carbonates are pushed deep under the surface of the earth, they decompose, releasing carbon dioxide as gas once again.

And how does that carbon dioxide get back to the surface and into the atmosphere again? Anybody like to guess? . . . Through volcanoes! As they erupt, huge amounts of carbon dioxide are spewed back into the air.

The earth itself is a vast recycling machine. As carbon dioxide takes part in processes that are essential to life on earth, it gets locked away. But then the very structure of our planet recycles the carbon dioxide and releases it as gas again. Earthquakes happen because of that recycling, and volcanoes are an essential part of the process.

That process is one of the wonders of planet earth. It is one of the many reasons some scientists believe that there had to be a Creator God to design earth so precisely for life to be possible.

A thought and a prayer

We still have big questions about the problem of death and suffering through natural disasters, but at least we now know that even earthquakes and volcanoes have their place. They are essential for our very existence here on earth. We might want to pray something like this:

Creator God, thank you for the ways science helps us to understand the world you made for us to live in. Please help scientists and governments to make the right discoveries and decisions so that less suffering is caused by natural disasters. Amen.

NOTE

For more on a similar theme, see *77 Talks for 21st Century Kids*, "BUZZ OFF!" p. 145 and "Creepy-crawly or doctor's friend?" p. 163.

58
You've been framed!

Theme

The need for forgiveness.

You will need

- an old video cassette, a hammer and a waste bin.

Presentation

Show the video cassette (or, if you have a camcorder, you could start by videoing the children).

Did you hear about the two burglars who videoed themselves committing crimes? They filmed each other breaking into houses, smashing up buildings and committing burglaries — more than 30 crimes in all. Then they carefully edited their tapes, adding subtitles and background music.

They reckoned without a visit from the police. Tamworth CID in Staffordshire were doing a routine search while investigating a completely unrelated matter. They noticed the videos, and their suspicions were aroused by the titles. When the men tried to keep them away from the police, it confirmed their suspicions.

So Tamworth police had a complete video record of a minor local crime wave. Guess who pleaded guilty when the case came to court!

Most sane people want to keep their wrongdoings well hidden, not make a film of them. Pause for a moment and think of some of the things each one of us would absolutely hate to have recorded on video for public show . . . Painful!

God is not a policeman

In one of his letters in the New Testament, Paul wrote:

> **Each of us will have to answer to God for what he has done.** *Romans 14:12*

We don't have to be stupid enough to video our own foolishness — God is outside time and space and knows everything we have ever done. There is a record of our lives from start to finish. That is not because God is a big policeman in the sky, waiting to catch people. He simply knows everything.

Perhaps that's a good reason for taking seriously that bit in the Lord's Prayer that says, "Forgive us the wrongs we have done." Forgiveness means wiping the tape clean, erasing the record, making a new beginning.

[You could smash the video cassette at this point for dramatic effect, or simply throw it in a bin.]

But it is not a magic formula: we have to be genuinely sorry for what we have done and determined not to do it again. There's also that bit about forgiving other people for what they have done to us: we have to be prepared to let go of the "video" records we have in our heads of how other people have hurt us.

Do we want the record to stand? Or do we want it wiped away so we can make a fresh start? Those two criminals didn't have that choice. Jesus teaches us that *we* do.

Something to do

Everyone, including leaders, could privately write on a piece of paper something they are sorry for, and then throw it in the bin.

59
A close shave

Theme

A fun beginning leads to some serious reflection on what is involved when we pray, "Forgive us our sins."

You will need

- a bowl of water, a towel, shaving foam, safety and cut-throat razors (borrow the latter from a barber if necessary).
- for a fun ending if you wish, two identical buckets and a packet of confetti. Empty the confetti into one of the buckets and hide this in advance behind the table you will use.

Presentation

Announce that you have decided to take up a new trade and that you are sure the group is going to help you get started, by allowing you to practise on them. You are going to be a barber and you are going to start with the easy bit — shaving someone. If a parent doesn't volunteer, get the children to choose a "volunteer". (For a school assembly, prime a teacher.) Tell him to sit down; put the towel round his neck. Get the foam, and spray it liberally on him. Then show him the cut-throat razor, and do a bit of patter on how easy it looks, even though you have never tried using a cut-throat razor before. When sufficient effect has been created, the safety razor is produced (usually with its cover still on) so that you will lightly take off the foam and finish the "shave". Then pour the water into the empty bucket and put it down out of sight behind the table.

Tell the boys that when they grow up, shaving will be a daily routine (unless they grow a beard). And whether we need to shave or not, washing or showering is a daily must for everyone. (Boys may not agree with this!) We all have something else that needs dealing with on a daily basis. When Jesus' followers asked him to teach them how to pray, he gave them the model we call the Lord's Prayer. One of the things it includes is, "Forgive us our sins as we forgive those who sin against us."

Blob of meanness

Like whiskers or dirt, sin builds up every day. A smear of selfishness here, a stain of untruth there, an ugly blob of meanness . . . How do we clean away this sort of dirt? It won't wash off with soap; you can't scrape it off with even the sharpest razor. It is ingrained into the very fibre of our being. Sin needs a more powerful cleanser — and there is only one place you can get it.

Several times in the Bible there is a word-picture of Jesus which includes something strange. For example, in the first chapter of the book of Revelation, verses 15 and 16 describe Jesus like this:

His feet were like bronze that glows hot in a furnace. His voice was like the noise of flooding water. He held seven stars in his right hand. A sharp two-edged sword came out of his mouth. He looked like the sun shining at its brightest time.

A sharp two-edged sword coming out of his mouth? It sounds odd, but remember this is a word-picture. This is a symbol, a way of saying that the words that come out of Jesus' mouth are powerful. With a word he created the universe. With a word he can strike down a whole nation.

One time, some friends brought a paralyzed man to Jesus. Jesus healed him, but first he said,

Son, your sins are forgiven. *Mark 2:5*

The religious leaders were furious. They knew that only God has the power to forgive sins. But Jesus was God. The words of his mouth had the power to clean that man inside-out.

So when we pray, "Forgive us our sins", we are asking for something much more powerful, much sharper than this cut-throat razor, to clean us up. We are asking God to say the words to us, **"Your sins are forgiven."**

When I showed *John* [your volunteer] this razor, he was scared. And he was right to be scared! It's dangerous. And we are right to fear the sharp two-edged sword that comes out of the mouth of Jesus — the words that have power to create or to destroy. The wonder of it is, no matter what we may have done, when we come to Jesus genuinely wanting to be right with him, he uses that sharp sword so gently that he removes all the wrong from us and leaves us clean and whole and unharmed.

Prayer

A time of quiet would be appropriate here for people to bring anything to Jesus they want to say sorry for and, perhaps, to imagine him as in the word-picture from Revelation.

Fun ending

Pick up the bucket containing the confetti. Hold it up so that people can see — they will think it is the bucket with the water in it. Swish it round, wander down the middle of your audience, trip and throw the bucket full of confetti into the gathering. They will part like the Red Sea!

60
Daydreaming

Theme

Research shows that daydreaming may not be such a bad thing after all. The reaction of Nathanael when Jesus said he had seen him under the fig-tree (John 1:47–49) suggests that the young man may have been doing a spot of divinely-inspired daydreaming.

You will need

* to read the story in John 1:43–51.

Presentation

Hands up — who has ever got into trouble for daydreaming in class? . . .

Is it just *some* people who daydream, while others get on with the job in hand undistracted? Is daydreaming a bad thing, a waste of time? (You might describe one of your own favourite daydreams.)

It would probably surprise most of us to know that the average person spends more than one third of their waking hours daydreaming. We actually spend more of our waking hours daydreaming than we spend of our time asleep in night-dreaming. Our daydreams can be anything from a passing thought to a full-blown reverie that lasts a few minutes. It is the last that gets us into trouble when we are supposed to be concentrating on our maths!

It has been shown that daydreaming has some quite beneficial effects. It helps us to relax, and sometimes it even lowers our blood pressure. It can be quite helpful if you have a problem to solve, and it can also be creative, so daydreaming in class might not always be a waste of time, after all.

A bit of a hero

There was a young man in the Bible who was doing a spot of daydreaming one time. His name was Nathanael, and he had found a nice spot to daydream on a hot Mediterranean spring day — underneath a shady fig-tree. His daydream was like many of ours: imagining ourselves a bit of a hero, being centre stage in some important event. It looks as though he was daydreaming about being a real top-of-the-class Israelite and being a bit like Israel himself, the man from whom the nation took its name. Israel himself had a dream in which he saw heaven open and God's messengers — angels — going up and down between earth and heaven. (Genesis 28:10–15. This was before his name was changed from Jacob to Israel — see Genesis 32:28.)

While Nathanael was in the middle of this daydream, one of his friends turned up, Philip. Philip insisted on taking him to see someone he had just met, Jesus of Nazareth. Nathanael was a bit cross at being disturbed — daydreamers will know how he felt! But when he met Jesus he was in for a big shock. Jesus told him exactly what he had been daydreaming about under the fig-tree. Not only that, but Jesus said his daydream was going to come true! He would see angels. "I tell you the truth," said Jesus to his new friends. "You will all see heaven open. You will see 'angels of God going up and coming down' on the Son of Man." (By "Son of Man" Jesus meant himself.)

And Nathanael did see remarkable things. At the end of John's story of Jesus, we learn that Nathanael was with some of the other disciples when Jesus appeared on the beach at the Sea of Galilee after his resurrection. (See John 21:2.) Imagine being one of the people who saw Jesus after he came back from the dead!

So try a spot of daydreaming. Unplug the telly, switch off the mobile, stretch out somewhere comfortable and enjoy the pictures inside your head. Remember Nathanael. You never know what it might lead to!

Something to do

If the children are in the mood, you could finish with some quiet music and a couple of minutes' quiet "daydreaming time".

61
Blind man sees

THEME

Asking God to guide our dreams. This could follow on from "Daydreaming".

You will need

- a stick, a piece of cloth for a cloak, a bowl, some coins.
- to prepare the story of Bartimaeus in Luke 18:35–43.
  (Luke does not tell us his name, but Mark does. It means
  Son of Timaeus.)

Presentation

Tell the story as an impromptu drama, recruiting
volunteers to play different parts as you go along.

[Set the scene.] Jericho is a town just north of the Dead
Sea. It is extremely hot there most of the year, but springs
provide water, and tall palm trees carry great bunches of
bright red and yellow dates. In Jesus' time, the main trade
route from Arabia to Damascus passed through the town.
Caravans of laden camels arrived regularly. There was a
tax-collection booth and a large Roman garrison.

Ask for a volunteer to be Bartimaeus. Describe him sitting
on his cloak in the shade of a palm tree, with his begging
bowl in front of him. Get a couple of children to drop
coins in his bowl.

Bartimaeus had plenty of time for daydreaming. Ask for
suggestions as to the kind of daydreams he might have
had (e.g. good food . . . a rich merchant giving him a big
gift . . . getting his sight back).

Jesus was on his way to Jerusalem. He had walked down the road beside the river Jordan from Galilee. From Jericho he would begin the long, hot climb uphill to the capital. Have more volunteers play the parts of Jesus, his disciples, and the people in the crowd, as you tell the rest of the story.

Getting his sight restored meant big changes for Bartimaeus. He would have to stop begging and start working. What kind of work would he do? There would be all kinds of things other people had done for him or helped him with, that now he would have to do for himself. He was praising God, but his new life would not be easy.

Something to think about

We need to think carefully about our daydreams and what it would mean if they came true. Jesus asked Bartimaeus what he wanted and then gave him what he asked for. Perhaps the best thing we can do is to ask God to guide our daydreams, so that what we dream about is what he knows is best for us.

62
Surgical trust

Theme

For a bit of fun, here is a list of things you would not want to hear if the anaesthetic started to wear off and you began to come round on the operating table. We finish with a prayer of thanks for the real-life skills of the medical profession.

You will need

- For the best effect, the two unseen readers, A and B, speak into microphones with some echo on. Someone else holds another mike with a cloth wrapped round it and beats a heartbeat throughout. Leave time between each line for the penny to drop and — hopefully — laughter.
- To add atmosphere, a little disinfectant could be sprinkled around before you start.

Presentation

This morning, we are going to take you on a journey into a nightmare. We want you to imagine that you are in hospital. Today they are taking you down for an operation. You are going to hear a number of things you might find rather disturbing. Is it just a dream . . . or are you coming round without anyone realizing?

[Dim the lights. Put on a "hypnotic" voice.] Now, close your eyes and breathe in that hospital smell. The injection is starting to work and you are feeling drowsy. A nurse wheels you on the trolley into the theatre. Green smocks and white masks surround you as you stare up at the lights and the anaesthetic mask comes down over your mouth and nose. "Breathe deeply," says a faraway voice, "and count slowly to ten." The last thing you hear is the beating of your heart [start "heartbeat" on microphone] . . . and your own voice counting, "One . . . two . . . three . . ." At least, that's the last thing you hear *until the anaesthetic starts to wear off* . . .

A Welcome to the team, Doctor. What did you say your name was? . . . Frankenstein?

(Boom . . . boom . . . boom . . .)

B Did you mean to cut quite that deep, Doctor? You've come right out the other side!

A This is the first time I've tried this keyhole surgery. Er, anyone know what to do when you lose the key?

B Good heavens! That's bigger than the one they've got in the Science Museum!

A Rover! Rover! . . . Bring that back! . . . You bad dog!

B If the England team can lose three on the trot, nobody can blame me for losing the odd one!

A Anyone got a pen? See if you can bring him round quick. I want him to sign a donor card.

B For heaven's sake, be careful, Nurse! Now you've got blood all over it and I can't read the next bit of the instructions!

A Can't somebody stop that thing beating? It's getting on my nerves.

B Unt now ve remove ze subject's brain . . . unt ve place it in ze body of ze ape.

PRESENTER OK, you can wake up now. It was just a bad dream. As we breathe a sigh of relief, perhaps we could say a prayer of thanks for the real-life skill and dedication of the medical and support staff in our hospitals and at the local doctor's surgery.

A prayer

Father God, our bodies are wonderful, and complex, and mysterious. Thank you that for so much of the time we can take them for granted, as long as we give them food and drink and rest. But when something goes wrong, or we have an accident, thank you for the skills and knowledge that so often allows us to be made well again. Amen.

Expert Futurologists

The future is bright — if we know
how to prepare for it

63
Planning for
the future

Theme

Why the Bible is the best guide to the future.

You will need

- a pocket Bible.

Presentation

Futurologists are people who look at current trends and research, and project them into the future. These are some of their ideas about what they expect to become reality during your lifetime:

2006 You are lying back on your bed, eyes closed, researching your homework by surfing the Web. No, it's not a dream. You have contact lenses that are linked to the Internet. You can surf the Web without even opening your eyes.

2007 You walk to your car and it opens the doors without you lifting a finger. The radio automatically tunes to your favourite station. You arrive home and your house sees you come in. It flashes your e-mails up on a screen. How? You have a whole PC under your skin, complete with microprocessor and memory, powered by radio waves. It automatically communicates with your car, your house, your office, your phone, or the cash machine at the bank.

2008 Carry a spare sweater in your bag in case it goes cold? No need. You are wearing clothes made of smart fabric. They are programmed to warm up when you get cold, or cool down if you get too hot.

2010 "Rover! Bring me my slippers. And while you are at it, cook me a pizza, open me a beer, and run my dirty washing through the machine." No problem. Your robotic pet understands every word you say. And it never makes a mess on the carpet.

2016 Dring, dring! It's Uncle Phil from Australia. He's standing in the middle of your living room with his surfboard, wishing you a merry Christmas. Well, his holographic image is, anyway.

2018 Schools drop foreign languages. All language teachers find themselves out of a job. Automated translators allow people to talk freely with others speaking different languages.

2020 There are 1 billion elderly people — over the age of 60 — in the world. Three quarters of them live in developing countries with little in the way of pensions.

2030 You want to order the week's groceries? Just think. Change the TV channel? Just think. Send an e-mail to your business associate in China? Just think. The computer linked directly to your brain does it all at the speed of thought.

These are just a few of the things we can foresee coming. If past experience is any guide, then some of these will fall by the wayside, while other things will develop in totally unexpected ways.

Not many years ago, one of the top computer experts of the time could not see a reason why anyone would want a computer in their home. Now, many of us could not live without them. As plenty of other people have found to their cost, predicting the future can leave you with a lot of egg on your face!

Predictions proved true

I have in my pocket the most useful guide to the future available anywhere in the world. It has the great advantage of having been around long enough for many of its predictions to have been proved true. It doesn't cover everything, but it does deal thoroughly with the most important things. Here it is: **a Bible.**

There are two reasons why I trust it, and two reasons why it is the most useful guide to have.

Reason number one for trusting it This I've already mentioned: it contains hundreds of predictions, many written centuries before they happened, that have come true. A great many of those predictions were about Jesus.

Reason number two I believe it is inspired by God, and God is outside time, so he knows the future.

Reason number one why it is the most useful guide to have Technology may change, but human nature doesn't. This is where past experience is the most valuable guide we have. And the Bible is the best guide to human experience in the world.

Reason number two The most important thing for *me* to know about my future is what will happen to me when I leave this planet. And I mean, leave it in a coffin, not in a spaceship to Mars. This book tells me. And it tells me how to plan for the future beyond the future.

Not bad for a book that costs a couple of quid and you can slip in your pocket. Be an expert futurologist: get a Bible.

NOTE

For the latest in future predictions, check out the World Future Society at http://www.wfs.org/index.htm.

64
Like him

Theme

**A glimpse into that amazing future when we shall see Jesus
— and find that we are like him.**

You will need

- There is an easy option and a time-consuming option. See
  below for the former. For the latter, it is probably best to get
  a computer-literate young person to do it for you! You need
  some familiar faces — either from scanned photos of
  people in your group or of people known to them, or from,
  for example, a TV magazine. These should have effects
  applied to them in a photo programme to make them hard
  to recognize, for example, artistic effects. Finally, they need
  to be printed on transparencies or prepared to show on a
  computer screen.
- Easy option. Print out some historical characters from
  www.77talks.co.uk.

Presentation

Get volunteers or the whole group to guess who the people
are in the doctored photos. Or divide the group into teams
and let them do it competitively.

Comment on how easy — or how hard — it has been to
recognize the faces in the photos. If we know a face well,
we can often recognize it in even a badly distorted picture.

One face people have wanted to see down the centuries is
the face of Jesus. Many artists have painted him, but
nobody actually knows what he looked like. There is no
description of his human appearance in the Bible.

It seems from reading the Bible that what Jesus looked like when he was here on earth doesn't really matter. What does matter is what he is like as a person. And we can know that. We can know that by reading about him in the gospel stories, by talking to him in prayer, by being his follower, his disciple, his apprentice. There is no doubt then that we shall know him when we see him.

But one of the people who did know what he looked like, John, one of his first disciples, says something strange about that moment when we see him as he really is. He says we shall be like him! Listen to this:

Have a child read **1 John 3:1–3**.

Something to think about

John says that we have not yet been shown what we will be like in the future. That is still a mystery. But we are going to be like Jesus! When we think about Jesus, we think about his amazing love, his infinite wisdom, his unbelievable power that created the universe. He is perfect, pure, glorious — and yet he is the closest and best friend anyone ever had. And we are going to be like him. Just how, we don't know yet. It's like the biggest Christmas present you ever dreamed of, waiting to be unwrapped. It is a mystery — but what an exciting mystery! No wonder John exclaims, **"The Father has loved us so much! He loved us so much that we are called children of God."**

So treasure this thought in your heart: "One day I am going to see my Lord, the King of kings, the Son of God. I am going to see Jesus as he really is. And when I see him, I am going to be like him. Wow!"

65
Purpose in all
that we do

Theme

When we see a purpose in all we do, every part of our lives becomes valuable.

You will need

- some pieces of paper with numbers written on them as shown here.
- an OHP, an acetate with the sum below, a pen, and a prize of some kind.

Presentation

You need to do the first part of this talk one week — it only takes a couple of minutes — and the main part the following week.

Week 1

(This can be at the end of another talk.) Announce that you have something valuable to give away. In fact, you have ten (or more) of them to give away freely to people who want them.

```
2
8
5
3
9
```

Give out the pieces of paper with these five numbers on. When children ask why they are valuable, simply say that hopefully they will find out sometime. Tell them to do what you usually do with something valuable: keep it safe. Refuse to say any more.

Week 2

Announce that you have a prize which — hopefully — is going to be won by someone in the room. Show the prize.

Display an acetate showing a sum with missing numbers on the OHP, as shown below. Explain that it is a simple addition sum, but some of the numbers are missing. There are several possible combinations of numbers that would fit, but you are looking for one particular set of numbers. Provide a pen. The first person who can come and write in the missing numbers will win the prize.

```
  7 3 _ 5 9
  4 0 _ 4 6
  3 6 _ 0 4
+ 9 5 _ 7 2
2 4 5 _ 8 1
```

What happens at this moment is unpredictable. Perhaps someone will realize quickly that the missing numbers are on the pieces of paper that you gave out last week. Or it may need a little prompting. If nobody has the numbers with them, the prize will have to wait until someone brings it.

Hold up a copy of the original piece of paper. It doesn't look much. It has no value on its own and is totally uninteresting. We had to wait a week to find out what its value was. There are lots of things in life which are like that. There are lessons at school which do not interest us much and do not seem to have much purpose. There are things our parents ask us to do which we find boring. We may have to wait a long time before we find out their real value.

There is a secret, known to some Christians, that can turn any lesson, any job, into something valuable. A poet who was born more than 400 years ago knew the secret and wrote it in a poem that is also a prayer. His name was George Herbert.

Teach me, my God and King,
In all things Thee to see,
And what I do in any thing
To do it as for Thee.

In this poem George Herbert is praying to see God in everything. Because he knows God created the world and

everything in it with a purpose, he knows that nothing is
without value or without meaning. If we do everything as
though it was God himself teaching us or telling us what
to do, then every single part of our lives becomes valuable.
Everything becomes like this piece of paper — a thing of
value to be stored up until its worth becomes clear.

A prayer

Read the words of the poem again as a prayer that the
children can join in with, if they want to make it their
own.

66
Growing into responsibility

Theme

Taking on larger responsibilities is an essential part of growing up. It's God's plan, too.

You will need

- two prepared OHP transparencies; coloured pens. Draw a table as in the model (see p. 228) or print it from the *www.77talks.co.uk* website. In the left-hand column, list responsibilities appropriate to the age of the group. For under-11s, for example, *Chores at home, Keep bedroom tidy, Run errands, Look after pets, Thank you letters, Register or dinner monitor*, etc. For over-11s, some of the above plus: *Babysitting, Clothing allowance, Caring for ill parent, Part-time job, Music practice, Team captain*, etc. Prepare a second table with responsibilities suitable for the next phase of life, i.e. for under-11s make an over-11s table; for over-11s make a young adult table. Leave some rows blank.
- Prepare to tell the parable of the three servants, **Matthew 25:14–30**. The *Good News Bible* is a helpful basic translation, but both *The Living Bible* and *The Message* have some great lines. Avoid the misleading word "talents".

Presentation

Display the chart appropriate to the age-group and ask for a volunteer. Work down the left-hand column, looking at the different responsibilities, and asking the volunteer to say whether he or she has no responsibility in that area, or some, or a lot, or too much. Colour in the chart accordingly. If there are blank rows, children might suggest other ways in which some of them carry responsibility. Ask how they feel about these responsibilities. Good? Proud? Too much bother? . . .

Responsibility	None	Some	A lot	Too much
Jobs in school				
Keep room tidy				
Run errands				
Look after pet(s)				

Ask for some suggestions as to what extra or increased responsibilities they expect to take on in the next few years. After a few suggestions, show your second table. Point out the ideas you had, and add any others they indicated. Are they looking forward to some of these new responsibilities? Or scared about some of them? . . .

A major part of growing up is taking on more responsibility. It began when we first took responsibility for putting the food in our own mouths instead of Mum feeding us, and it has been increasing in large and small steps ever since. Big ones in the future include things like driving a car, living on your own, getting married, starting a family. As a general rule, increased responsibility at work means a bigger pay-packet. New responsibilities can be exciting, but they can also be scary and time-consuming. Ducking them is like saying you don't want to grow up.

Jesus told a famous story about some people rising to the challenge of new responsibilities — and one who didn't.

Retell the parable of the three servants from **Matthew 25:14–30**.

Draw out the contrast. For the first servant, one translation reads:

His master praised him for good work. "You have been faithful in handling this small amount," he told him, "so now I will give you many more responsibilities. Begin the joyous tasks I have assigned to you."

verse 21, The Living Bible

But as for the third:

"That's a terrible way to live! It's criminal to live cautiously like that!" *verse 26*, The Message

It seems that growing into more and more responsibility is part of God's plan for human beings. And for those ready to take on responsibilities willingly, he has planned big-time rewards. Who knows, you might even end up being responsible for a whole galaxy!

67
How will you
manage your £1m?

Theme

**A surprising message on being streetwise from perhaps
Jesus' most "difficult" parable: the story of the crooked
manager. The figures are obviously approximate, but broadly
realistic.[1]**

You will need

- a board or OHP and pens.
- Luke 16:1–9 in *The Message* (Peterson's version provides
  an illuminating commentary on this passage).

Presentation

Ask the children how much they think they will earn
during their lifetime . . . On average earnings at today's
rate it will be something like £1 million. With inflation
this means that everyone will earn well over that — and
some people very much more.

How much will you spend, and on what? . . . (Write figures
on OHP.) About a quarter will go on taxes of various kinds
— say £250,000.

Housing: at least £200,000.

Living: (food, transport, entertainment, clothes, etc.) —
£320,000.

Pension: (everyone will have to buy their own) —
£130,000.

What does this add up to? £900,000.

That leaves £100,000. This could go on a bigger house, better holidays — or something else you choose. We'll leave that to think about later.

£1 million	
Tax	£250,000
Housing	£200,000
Living	£320,000
Pension	£130,000
Sub-total	£900,000
? ? ?	£100,000

Good managers

If you went for a job that involved handling £1m you would certainly be expected to be a good manager. As each of us is really going to handle at least that much in our lives, we *all* need to be good managers. Jesus told a story that had some surprising advice on how to handle our money.

Read **Luke 16:1–9** in *The Message*, then reinforce the main lines of the story to make sure the children understand.

Jesus wasn't suggesting that we should be crooks. He was advising us to use what we have wisely, in order to plan for our future. Wise people know they have to put some money aside for a pension — even though it's a lifetime away for people of your age.

Long-term future

People who are even wiser know that they should be planning for life beyond this life. If life on earth is just episode 1 of something much greater, then the future beyond the future needs some thought, too. One thing many Christians do is to take 10% of their earnings [point to the £100,000 on the OHP] and give it away. They look for opportunities to use that money in ways that will really help other people in need. Jesus talked about this as "storing up treasure in heaven". As he says here (in a different translation): **"Make friends for yourselves with worldly wealth, so that when it gives out, you will be welcomed in the eternal home."**

Most of the people we help with our money will probably never know us personally, but God knows. The money we give away is banked for us — in heaven.

So enjoy your £1 million. But be a bit streetwise with it. Invest some in your long-term future — the future beyond the future.

NOTE

1 Originally, every third year, the tithe of the harvest was kept in storehouses for distribution to the poor and needy (see Deuteronomy 14:22–29). Taxation could be seen as partially accomplishing this end today. On this basis you might want to adjust the figures to leave £75,000 rather than £100,000.

68
Bumps on the head

Theme

One discredited "science" opens the door for a little undermining of the modern equivalents of explaining human behaviour and telling the future — astrology and palmistry.

You will need

- You could use the phrenology picture from the *www.77talks.co.uk* website.

Presentation

Ask the children to feel their heads and note where there are bumps on their skulls. If the group won't get out of hand, they could feel their neighbour's head and do a comparison.

Do bumps in different places tell you something about your abilities or your character? People in the 19th century thought they did.

It was an Austrian doctor, Franz Gall, who first proposed the idea. He believed that if you were good at music, for example, the music-centre in your brain would be larger than normal and cause a bump at a particular place on your skull. Being good at maths would cause a bump somewhere else.

It wasn't just skills that the bumps were supposed to show. Gall thought they could provide a guide to the kind of person you were. A bump in one place might show, for example, that you would love your children. A bump somewhere else might show that you were likely to be a thief.

233

The name given to this study of personality through bumps on the head was *phrenology*.

Phrenology became hugely popular in Europe and America. Queen Victoria of England was one of the people to believe in it. Books and leaflets were published. Models and pictures of the head were produced, showing the areas linked to different abilities. Some people made lots of money out of it.

One of the reasons it was so popular was that it seemed to give a scientific explanation for the way people behaved. People who were losing interest in the church liked that. Instead of saying, "I've done something wrong. I'm sorry", you could say, "It's not my fault. It's just the way I'm made. The bumps on my head show that."

History of ignorance

These days we know that Franz Gall was completely wrong. Brain-scanning machines show that the brain is an amazingly complex web of connections. There is no simple pattern of different parts controlling different activities. And there is absolutely no link whatsoever between the bumps on your head and the kind of person you are.

Very few people believe in phrenology today. It is just part of the history of ignorance. We wouldn't be so silly as to be taken in by anything like that today. Or would we?

What about astrology — "Your future in the stars" — or palmistry, or other kinds of fortune-telling? Aren't they very similar? They claim to be able to tell your character by the time and place you were born or by the lines on your hand. And there is lots of money to be made by selling books and writing newspaper columns on "your stars".

There seems to be an awful lot of people around who don't want to take responsibility for their own choices or actions. They would much rather believe that things can be explained by their stars, or their tarot card readings, or something similar.

Centuries and centuries ago people knew that astrology was a waste of time. Isaiah, one of the prophets whose words we have in the Bible, said:

> **You have advisors by the ton — your astrologers and stargazers, who try to tell you what the future holds. But they are as useless as dried grass burning in the fire.** *Isaiah 47:13–14*, The Living Bible

So why do people go on believing in them? Well, here's one theory. Maybe they had a bump on the head when they were children!

Seasons of Good Cheer

However far we may travel in cyberspace, we will never lose the need to respond to the rhythm of the seasons. The great stories of the Christian calendar mark those seasons indelibly

69
Voice from
the heavens

Theme

Will aliens give us the answer to all our problems? Or have we already heard the authentic voice from the heavens?

You will need

- to read the story of the transfiguration of Jesus in Mark 9:2–8.
- sci-fi pictures of aliens, or use the cartoon at *www.77talks.co.uk*.

Presentation

Who knows what the SETI programme is? A clue: it is run by American astronomers and you probably know what the letters ET stand for . . .

Answer: the Search for Extra-Terrestrial Intelligence.

This search is being carried out using radio-telescopes. Researchers are looking at stars similar to our own sun and hoping to pick up the same kind of radio signals that we produce on our own planet. If there are advanced alien civilizations out there, then they should be communicating with each other by radio and we should be able to listen in. People can use their own computers to join in the search through the SETI@home project. This runs on screen-savers on home computers to check out samples of signals received by radio-telescopes.

The Encyclopedia Galactica

The cost of the American SETI Institute's project is $4–5 million per year. Some of the people who are helping to pay for the search hope that any extra-terrestrials we make contact with will be kind enough to beam us a copy of what they call the *Encyclopedia Galactica*, a book with the answers to all the world's problems.

[Here's an interesting thought: What might we send them in return? What do you give to beings who already know all there is to know?]

Before we get too excited at the prospect, we ought to consider a few things:

1 Despite several years of listening to stars in our galactic neighbourhood, not a single intelligent bleep has been heard.

2 The nearest likely stars are at least 100 light-years from earth. That means that if anything were to be detected, it would take around 200 years to send the ETs a "Hello, we're your friendly neighbours" message and get a reply. There will be no *Encyclopedia Galactica* during our lifetime, nor even the lifetime of our great-great-great-great-great-grandchildren.

Turning a deaf ear

3 There is other scientific research that the SETI enthusiasts would rather not hear. This suggests that the earth could be the only planet in the whole Milky Way galaxy which can support life. Indeed, it may be the only life-supporting planet in the whole universe. There are so many factors that have to be just right for a planet to support life that the chance of finding such a planet is incredibly small. (For one example, see the carbon dioxide balance featured in "Volcanoes and earthquakes".)

So do we give up all hope of receiving a message from the heavens that will give us the answer to our problems? Well, maybe not. Maybe some people have already heard it, and without millions of dollars' worth of high-tech equipment.

Tell the story of the transfiguration in **Mark 9:2–8**.

The voice said, **"This is my Son, whom I love. Listen to him!"** People had heard a voice saying similar words when Jesus was baptized in the river Jordan.

Something to think about

The most serious problems on this planet are not the ones that any *Encyclopedia Galactica* might give us the answer to. They are the human failings inside each one of us: greed, selfishness, jealousy, etc. Christians believe we already have a book that shows us the answers to those problems: the Bible. And they believe that the voice the disciples heard, the voice of God, gives us the best message from "out there" that we will ever receive: **"This is my Son, whom I love. Listen to him!"**

NOTE

For more facts and the latest information from the ET searchers go to www.seti.org.

70
Jesus or Barabbas?

Theme

A theme for Easter: the choice between the way of violence and the way of peace.

You will need

- some details of a conflict situation in the news.

Presentation

Talk about a war or terrorist situation that is in the news. The children might be asked if they know about other violent conflicts that are going on.

Disagreement, argument and conflict are bound to happen. We all disagree with other people, usually several times a day. When an argument becomes very heated, there may come a moment when one of the sides chooses to become violent. In every war we read about or see on the TV news, such a choice has been made.

The Palm Sunday coup

The Easter story gives us a dramatic account of some people making a choice like that. Jesus arrived in Jerusalem on Palm Sunday. The people welcomed him like a king. He went to the temple and threw out the money-changers. Crowds flocked to hear him in the temple precincts during that week.

In a sense, Jesus took over the temple. He showed that the rulers of Jerusalem and the temple had lost the right to be moral and spiritual leaders. But he did it non-violently. On Palm Sunday, Jesus deliberately chose to enter the city on a humble donkey. This fulfilled the words that the prophet Zechariah had spoken more than 500 years earlier:

See, your king comes to you, gentle and riding on a donkey. *Zechariah 9:9* and *Matthew 21:5*

The way he came was gentle, non-violent.

Now listen to what happened on the night of Thursday of that week when Jesus was arrested and brought before Pilate, the Roman governor.

Read or have children present **Matthew 27:15–26.**

This crowd was given a choice. They could choose Jesus, the man of peace, or Barabbas, the man of violence. These two men offered two different kinds of revolution. Jesus offered a new quality of life and a new way of living: the kingdom of heaven. Barabbas offered the way of armed rebellion against the Roman empire. The crowd made their choice — they chose freedom for the man of violence, and a violent death for the man of peace.

Horrific bloodbath

We can learn a lot from what happened later. Some groups continued to rebel against Rome. Around 40 years after the death of Jesus, Rome sent an army to put an end to the rebellions. The temple itself was destroyed in a horrific bloodbath as the Roman legions defeated the rebels.

Meanwhile, some people continued to follow the way of the man of peace, Jesus. These early Christians began to spread throughout the Roman empire. Sometime after 310 AD the Roman Emperor himself became a Christian. Now, nearly 20 centuries after that first Easter, followers of Jesus are counted in billions all over the globe. Which was more successful, the way of violence or the way of peace?

Something to think about

Sometime this week, perhaps today, we might get into an argument with someone. As we get more and more angry, we might be tempted to hit out — and hitting out can be with words as much as with fists. But before it gets too heated, we still have a choice. Which will we choose: the way of violence or the way of peace?

71
Who wants the lot?

Theme

A lively auction leads to thinking about why Jesus was prepared to pay the ultimate price on Good Friday.

You will need

- items to auction, suitable for your group (which could include stuff belonging to leaders that the children might regard as trophies); plenty of pennies; a suitable auctioneer's mallet, for example, a large inflatable one.

This should be fun, but it could also raise money for a cause you support. Tell the group in advance what you are planning. Bids only go up in pennies. Have a good supply of pennies and run a bureau de change before you start. Give some pennies to children who come unprepared so that they are not left out.

Presentation

Get a good, loud extrovert as the auctioneer and make it fast and noisy.

When the auction is in full swing, one of the leaders starts making extravagant bids for popular lots so that the children have no chance of getting them. After this has happened a few times, step in, drag the leader to the front, and ask the children what they think of him. Greedy? Selfish?

The auction could be finished with the greedy leader generally behaving but once or twice giving way to the temptation to outbid the children — and probably being shouted down for doing so.

Calm things down, perhaps with a song.

No limit

Now let's imagine an auction in which one bidder is
determined to get everything. He outbids everyone else, no
matter how high the bidding goes. He seems prepared to
pay anything, no limit. We would probably want to know
why. Does he have a special reason for wanting everything
on sale? Is he just a rich nutcase? Or is there an interesting
story that explains his strange behaviour?

Let's look at a case where something like this actually
happened.

Probably the most famous verse in the New Testament says,

> **For God loved the world so much that he gave his only
> Son. God gave his Son so that whoever believes in
> him may not be lost, but have eternal life.** *John 3:16*

God wants the lot. He wants every single person on the
face of the planet. He was prepared to pay whatever it cost.
So he sent Jesus, the Son, God in a human being. And
Jesus ends up dying a terrible death on a Roman cross!

So what's the story that explains God's strange behaviour?

Funny creatures

It's the story of a Creator who made a universe of a
hunded trillion stars so that one planet could exist with
some funny two-legged creatures: human beings. It's a
story of how he loved the creatures he made so much that
he wanted them to live for ever, to live with him in a place
beyond their dreams.

So that they could share that eternal life with him, he
made the funny two-legged creatures a lot like himself. He

gave them imagination and creativity and free choice. But some of the things they imagined, and some of the things they created, and some of the things they chose were destructive and evil. Every single one of the creatures was tainted, spoilt. They were unfit for the eternal life the Creator had planned for them. They were lost.

So what did he decide to do? Say it was all a mistake? Scrap the lot? Begin again? What would *you* do?

He wants the lot

Because he loved them so much, God found a way for his creatures to begin again — but without scrapping them. What was the way he found? **"God gave his Son so that whoever believes in him may not be lost, but have eternal life."** He sent Jesus. And Jesus paid the highest possible price for the funny two-legged creatures: he gave his life when he was crucified.

Was that greedy? No, just the opposite. It's the most generous thing imaginable. Jesus paid for our freedom, the freedom from our own mistakes and wrong choices. The freedom to live with him for ever in that place beyond our dreams. Satan may have had a claim on us. But Jesus outbid him. God does not want to lose even one of his funny creatures. He wants the lot.

72
Road to Emmaus

Theme

The Easter story of the disciples meeting Jesus on the road to Emmaus.

You will need

- some jelly babies, three clean yoghurt pots or plastic cups, and an OHP.

Presentation

Explain that you are going to demonstrate to the audience a trick which they can show to their family or friends. You need one volunteer.

Place three different coloured jelly babies on the OHP. (They won't need an OHP to do this at home; you are using it so everyone can see.) Cover them with the yoghurt pots.

Ask the volunteer to choose one of the pots, lift it up, and eat the jelly baby. Replace the pot where it was. Repeat with the other two jelly babies, keeping up suitable "patter", e.g. "You do realize these are *magic* jelly babies. I hope they don't turn you into a frog. Still, your friends probably couldn't tell the difference." "Do you want to check under that pot just to make sure the jelly baby has really gone?" etc.

Now ask the volunteer to choose one of the pots — but not to tell you which one yet — and concentrate really hard. In a moment everyone is going to see that the chosen pot is over all three jelly babies!

Ask the volunteer to point to her chosen pot. Make a bit of play about asking if she wouldn't rather have this other one; then give in, lift it up and *hold it on her head*. The pot is now over the three jelly babies! (Laughter all round — we hope!)

Ask for a round of applause for the volunteer.

Taken by surprise

Tell the audience that they were expecting one thing to happen, but something different happened instead. At the end, we were all taken by surprise, although what happened was quite obvious when we saw it. Sorry though, there was no magic!

There is a story about the first Easter in which two people had certain expectations about what was happening but got taken completely by surprise. In this story it looked as if there really was magic at the end, but it was something far more wonderful.

Tell the Emmaus Road story from **Luke 24:13–35**.

As you tell it, emphasize the elements which echo and contrast with the introduction:

- the expectations of the two which, in part, prevented them from realizing whom they had met. (It was also true that there was something "different" about Jesus after his resurrection.)
- the surprise of the revelation when they realized who had been talking to them.
- but this was no trick or magic: "The Lord really has risen from death!" The risen Jesus was able to appear and disappear at will. He appeared several times to his followers. Once, the Bible tells us, 500 people saw him at one time.

An unexpected ending to a trick can make us laugh. The unexpected ending to this story — and to the whole Easter story — excited the disciples so much that they devoted the rest of their lives to telling other people. It was a story that changed the world.

73
The Christmas watchers 1

Theme

This Christmas mini-series takes three groups of people who were watching and waiting — the shepherds, the Magi, and the worshippers at the temple — and asks questions about whom God speaks to and how he speaks.

You will need

- a wall display or OHP transparency as below. The two top lines are filled in ready; the other boxes can be written in or have prepared words stuck on at the appropriate moments. Decorate the chart to make it attractive.

THE CHRISTMAS WATCHERS		
Who were they?	What were they doing?	How did they hear God?
Men on the night shift	Working and wondering	Through a mega sound-and-light angel show

- For further visual impact, have a small group of children dressed as shepherds.
- A picture of the shepherds is available at *www.77talks.co.uk* in both full colour and outline (for children to colour themselves). This can be printed onto

thin card for children to take home and stand on the
mantelpiece or window ledge. Or they can find it on the
website and print it themselves. The other two groups of
watchers can be added in subsequent weeks.

Presentation

Ask the children how much time they spend on an average
day watching — watching TV, watching sport, or watching
a teacher showing them something . . . Watching is one
way of learning.

The first Christmas was a time when a few people who
were quietly watching found themselves caught up in the
most amazing events. There were three groups of watchers
who were all very different kinds of people and who heard
God speak to them in very different ways.

The first group of watchers were just ordinary working
men — the shepherds.

If you have a dressed-up group, bring them out. Ask the
children who the shepherds were . . . Fill in the first box:
Men on the night shift.

Near to Bethlehem was a tower on the road to Jerusalem. It
was called Migdal Eder, "the watch-tower of the flock".
This was where shepherds who were taking their flocks of
sheep for the sacrifices in the temple at Jerusalem spent
the night.

Big questions about life

If you are outside under the stars at night, what sort of
mood do you get into? [Sadly, many children will not have
experienced this, but you may still get some very
interesting answers.] . . . People often go quiet. They feel
small under the big night sky, but they may also feel
close to something important. It's a time when people

think about big questions about life and God and themselves.

The shepherds would have thought they were very humble people — not like the priests in the temple in Jerusalem where they were taking the sheep — but perhaps they were wondering whether God would ever use or talk to ordinary people like them.

On the chart, we put in the second box that they were working — because they were doing their daily task — but also that they were wondering.

What happened next? [Get the rest of the story from the children.] . . . This bunch of men who had never seen more than an oil-lamp or a fire at night were suddenly treated to 50 megawatts of angel power and a full heavenly sound-system! [Fill in the third column on the chart.] And they became the very first to see the Christ, the Messiah, the Saviour.

The Bible doesn't spell out exactly what they did then, but it is very likely that they finished their job by taking the sheep to Jerusalem — and telling everyone who would listen about the extraordinary things they had seen and heard.

> **. . . all who heard it were amazed at what the shepherds said to them.**
> *Luke 2:18*, New International Version

Probably some people thought that they had had too much to drink. But there was another group of watchers at the temple, and they would certainly have pricked up their ears with interest.

The Bible says,

The shepherds returned, glorifying and praising God for all the things they had heard and seen, which were just as they had been told.
Luke 2:20, New International Version

And the watchers at the temple? We'll find out about them next time.

74
The Christmas watchers 2

www.77talks.co.uk

Theme

For some reason Simeon and Anna (Luke 2:22–38) are almost invariably omitted from nativity plays. (Is it because they are less picturesque than the shepherds and wise men? Or is it ageism?) Yet they play a vital role in the story of the welcoming of the Messiah into the world.

You will need

* stage two of the Christmas watchers chart:

THE CHRISTMAS WATCHERS		
Who were they?	What were they doing?	How did they hear God?
Men on the night shift	Working and wondering	Through a mega sound-and-light angel show
Senior citizens	Waiting and worshipping	Through listening to other people and to the inner voice of the Holy Spirit

* You could print a photo of the Temple Mount in Jerusalem onto OHP transparency from the *www.77talks.co.uk* website.
* You could have two senior citizens dressed as Simeon and Anna. They might be prepared to talk about themselves in character and you could adapt the talk accordingly.

- A picture of Simeon and Anna for children is available at *www.77talks.co.uk*.

Presentation

Use the chart to recap briefly on the first group of watchers, the shepherds. Ask the children if they can remember where the shepherds may have taken their flocks after seeing the baby Jesus. . . . the Temple Mount in Jerusalem.

Show a picture of the Temple Mount if you have one. It was an amazing piece of engineering. King Herod extended it to the size of 32 football pitches and built the temple on it. (Today there is a mosque there, and the Dome of the Rock — a very holy place for Muslims.)

There were other watchers who came regularly to the Temple Mount. One of them was called Simeon and another was Anna. Anna was 84 and Simeon was an old man who knew he was nearing the end of his life.

[Fill in the first box: Senior citizens — or other appropriate term: the authors would say they were like themselves — wrinklies!]

Simeon and Anna were both Jews who were hoping to see the coming of the promised Messiah. In fact, the Holy Spirit had shown Simeon that he would see the Messiah before he died. For years they had waited for that day to arrive and had come regularly to the temple to worship God. [Fill in the second box.]

Only waiting

If we were to see a couple of old people slipping into a church on our way to school, we probably wouldn't think they were doing anything very important. But even though Simeon and Anna were only waiting and worshipping, God had plans that would make sure their names were remembered until the end of time.

God used a big "angel spectacular" to speak to the shepherds. But he used a completely different way to speak to Simeon and Anna, a way that he often uses to speak to people. We have already heard that the Holy Spirit had shown Simeon that he would see the Messiah. How had the Holy Spirit shown him that? Perhaps it was just a quiet inner voice.

Then there may have been something else as well. They may have heard the story of the baby in a manger that the shepherds told when they came to Jerusalem. If so, they would certainly have listened with excitement. They would have asked themselves, "Is this the time that God promised? Is this what we have been waiting for?" This is the kind of way God often works, using other people to confirm what the Holy Spirit has said to those who are watching and listening. [Complete the third box.]

Then the Holy Spirit spoke to Simeon again, or not so much spoke as gave him a nudge to go to the temple.

Imagine that huge area on the Temple Mount with hundreds of people milling around. There were priests, there were money-changers, there were traders selling animals for sacrifice, there were worshippers, there were scholars and teachers, there were beggars, and there were plenty of people with nothing much else to do but to hang around the place where all the action was.

And in the middle of all that bustle, there was a couple with a baby. They were just an ordinary couple, like many others who had brought their babies at 33 days old to present to the Lord God at the temple. It was just an ordinary baby, too, probably with a turned-up nose and a little black hair poking out of the cloths he was wrapped in. At least, he looked like an ordinary baby on the outside.

If this were a film, the camera would zoom in and focus on that little family, singling them out from the crowd. But there was no camera, just the Holy Spirit focussing the eyes of old Simeon on a man and a young woman and a baby — a family from up north, like the shepherds had talked about. It was Mary and Joseph and the month-old baby Jesus.

Die in peace

Simeon took the baby in his arms. With tears in his eyes, he thanked God that the promise had been kept. He had seen the Messiah, the Saviour. He could die in peace.

And as he was speaking to Mary and Joseph, someone else happened on the scene: 84-year-old Anna. She was just as excited, eager to tell all her friends who were hoping and praying the Messiah would come that this baby was *him*, the one the prophets had spoken about.

If our imaginary camera were to zoom slowly out again, we would see a little knot of people talking excitedly and beckoning others to join them. As we took in more of the scene, we would see that all over the rest of the Temple Mount it was just business as usual. The priests, the scholars, the traders, the beggars — they all had far more important things to do than to bother about a few doddering old wrinklies making a fuss about a couple of poor northerners and a baby. Funny how people can be so busy living that they miss what life is all about.

But for those who had watched for years, and waited for years, and worshipped for years, this was the most wonderful moment of their lives. They knew they were part of the biggest thing that had ever happened in the history of the world.

What they didn't know was that another group of watchers from far away was following a sign in the sky that was leading them to Jerusalem, too. You can probably guess who they are, but if not, we'll find out next time.

www.77talks.co.uk

75
The Christmas
watchers 3

Theme

The story of the Magi (Matthew 2:1–12) completes this Christmas mini-series and underlines how God speaks to all kinds of different people in different ways — if only we have our eyes and ears open expectantly.

You will need

- stage three of the Christmas watchers chart:

THE CHRISTMAS WATCHERS		
Who were they?	What were they doing?	How did they hear God?
Men on the night shift	Working and wondering	Through a mega sound-and-light angel show
Senior citizens	Waiting and worshipping	Through listening to other people and to the inner voice of the Holy Spirit
Researchers	Watching and working out	Through observations and enquiries

- As in talks 1 and 2 of the series, people could be dressed as the Magi.
- A picture of the Magi for children is available at *www.77talks.co.uk* to complete the set of Christmas watchers.

Presentation

Use the chart to recap briefly on the first two groups of watchers and how they heard God speaking to them.

Away to the east was another group of watchers who, like the shepherds, spent time out under the night sky. In a sense, it was their work too, except that what they were watching was not sheep but the sky itself. They watched the stars because they believed that the positions of the moving stars — what we now know to be the planets — could point to important events that were happening in the world.

Today, people like these who like old books and knowledge and trying to understand the world would be university professors or researchers. In those days they were known as Magi — "wise men". [Fill in the first box.]

As these men watched the sky, they may have seen some of the brightest stars — planets — coming close together. This is called a conjunction. From their books they worked out what it meant — that a new king of the Jews had been born. [Fill in the second box.] And then there was the moving star — a comet, perhaps? — that was to help them find where this new king had been born.

Old books tell the truth

What happened next? [Get the rest of the story from the children.] . . . These men were surprised not to find the new king of the Jews in the palace at Jerusalem. But they made enquiries, and King Herod's own wise men got out their old books which said that the Messiah would be born in Bethlehem. The star they had been following confirmed what the books said and left them in no doubt that this Jewish baby was the king they were seeking. No ordinary king, either. This was the long-promised Messiah. They bowed down and worshipped him.

So, quite differently from the shepherds at Bethlehem and the senior citizens in Jerusalem, these "wise men" heard God speak to them through their observations of the natural world and through the enquiries they made. [Fill in the final box.]

As we have been filling in our Christmas watchers chart, we have been doing some research of our own. And we have used an old book, too — the Bible. Our research shows us some interesting things. It shows us that God speaks to all kinds of different people: people doing ordinary jobs, people of all ages, people trying to understand the world. It shows us that they can be doing all sorts of different things: working, worshipping, watching, working out — even just waiting patiently. And it shows us that God can speak to us in all sorts of different ways: through angel messengers, or very quietly inside us, or through other people, or through books.

The lovely carol "O Little Town of Bethlehem" says:

How silently, how silently
The wondrous gift is given!
So God imparts to human hearts
The blessings of his heaven.

There were lots of people at that time hoping the Messiah, the Saviour, would come. There were many people at the temple who could have seen him in the arms of Mary and Joseph, but most of them were too busy to stop and wonder and ask questions — too busy living to find out what life is about. It was those who were quietly waiting and watching who discovered **"the wondrous gift"**. Will we be too busy this Christmas? Or will we be watching, hoping that God will speak to us, show us Jesus, and impart to our watching hearts the blessings of his heaven?

76
Inside-out Christmas

Theme

The way we retell the Christmas story, even in church, all too often brings it perilously close to a fairy story and obscures the reality of the God who identifies with the poor of the earth.

You will need

- to wear a couple of items of clothing you can take off, for example, a jacket and sweater or waistcoat. This works best if you are dressed smartly. Alternatively, appear with all your clothes on inside-out already.

Presentation

Silently take off the jacket. Hand it to a member of the "audience". Take off the waistcoat or sweater, turn it inside-out, and put it back on again. Do the same with the jacket. Dressed like this, present the message:

What a stupid thing to do — wear clothes inside-out! We've done the same with the Christmas story: turned it inside out. Like jackets, real-life events have an inside and an outside. The inside of events is the private things that happen, the thoughts people have, their feelings inside. The outside is what the neighbours see or what gets printed in the papers.

The Christmas story is like any other: it has an inside and an outside. But we've turned it all outside-in.

The *inside* of the story was that this baby was the Saviour whom people had been waiting for, for centuries. Men who listened to God had predicted where he was to be born, plus hundreds of things about his life and death. He was a very remarkable baby. But you couldn't see that from the outside.

And you wouldn't have seen the angels. At least, most people didn't. The heavenly choir chose to appear to a handful of men in the dead of night, well away from the big city. When was the last time you spent the night out of doors, sitting in a field?

Sugar icing

What we have done is to take those amazing but unseen parts of the story and lay them all over the outside, like sugar icing on a cake. That's why we decorate everything and make it colourful and glittery. It makes the whole thing look like a fairy story.

The real *outside* of the story, what most people would actually have seen, was very different.

You would have seen a very ordinary couple from a poor village where children often went hungry and many people were crippled or blinded from various diseases.

Then you would have seen the soldiers, because the country was occupied by a foreign army. And if you were around for any length of time, you would have seen the resistance fighters who had been caught, dying slow, agonizing deaths on crosses beside the roads.

And this couple had to make a long journey to another village for a census. She was pregnant. But you don't argue with the soldiers of an occupying power. When they got there, if they had had enough money, or weapons like the soldiers, they could have got a room. But they had neither weapons nor money.

The usual inside-out story shows them in a clean, rather

attractive stable. Have you ever been in a real, old-fashioned cow shed? It is filthy and it stinks.

No place for a baby

Actually, the Bible doesn't even mention a stable. It only talks about a feeding-trough, a manger. It was probably in a dark cave. What a place to have a baby!

And that reminds me of babies who are born on the streets and in shanty towns all over the Third World. Some of them spend all their lives on the street and die in the gutter.

That's why this story is so important: because Jesus knows what it is like to be a baby born in poverty. He was one of them. He knows what it's like to be one of the poor in a country occupied by foreign troops. He was one of them. He knows what it's like to be a refugee. He was one of them.

Which version of the story do you prefer? The pretty-pretty, sugar-coated, inside-out version for people who don't want to think too much?

Or the rough and dirty right-side-out version that says that God cares so much for the poor of the earth that he sent his own Son to be one of them?

Walk away quietly, having ensured in advance that whoever takes over at this point leaves a few moments of silence.

www.77talks.co.uk

77
Santa can't
but God can

Theme

A Christmas message that puts Santa Claus in his place. For use with older children, partly because of the content, but also because of the reactions of some parents to people tampering with childhood illusions.

You will need

- a Santa hat.
- You could use the cartoon at *www.77talks.co.uk*.

Presentation

Put on a Santa hat and tell the group that spoilsport scientists have brought poor old Santa Claus down to earth with a bump. Apparently someone at the Massachusetts Institute of Technology decided to put Santa's claims to the test. Then they spilled the beans by publishing the results on the Internet.

They worked out that Santa has to visit more than 90 million homes worldwide (not counting Muslims, Hindus and people of other faiths, because they have their own festivals). Racing round the world before the sun rises, Santa has just 1 thousandth of a second to climb down each chimney, fill stockings, and consume whatever mince pies and glasses of sherry have been left for him.

Although that is going to put him rapidly over the limit — can you be charged with drunk-driving a sleigh? — it's unlikely any police vehicle is going to be fast enough to catch and breathalyze him. Santa's sleigh is moving at

1,000 kilometres (625 miles) per second, or 3,000 times the speed of sound!

Super-strength reindeer

Then there is the problem of the weight of all those presents. With no more than one kilo (two pounds) for each child, that amounts to over 300,000 tonnes. Of course, Santa's reindeer are specially selected for the job, but even with super-reindeer ten times as strong as normal, it needs 214,200 of them to pull the sleigh.

This is where Santa gets into real difficulties. Including the weight of the reindeer, there are some 350,000 tonnes flying through the atmosphere at 1,000 kilometres (625 miles) per second. In the song, some people say Rudolf's nose glows bright red. This quickly comes true, as with the immense friction his nose rapidly changes from merely red to white-hot, and then poor Rudolf himself bursts into flame and vapourizes with a tremendous sonic boom. In less than 5 thousandths of a second, reindeer, sleigh, presents and Santa are no more than a fantastic fireworks display. This is as bad as the asteroid that put an end to the dinosaurs, so most of the people on earth are wiped out by the fireball and its global effects. Happy Christmas, everyone!

Impossible task?

In the past 150 years or so, Santa Claus has become an indispensable part of the celebrations of the birth of Jesus. But if Santa's task has been proved to be impossible, what about some of the claims for God and Jesus made in the Bible? For instance, what have scientists got to say about the claim that millions of people can talk to God — pray — all at the same time, and that God can listen to them all? That sounds very much like Santa's impossible task.

For this one, we have to go to what some scientists are saying about the very beginning of the universe.

According to one idea — known as string theory — in the first tiny fraction of a second of its existence the universe was expanding in ten dimensions. But almost immediately, six of those dimensions stopped expanding and remained incredibly tightly rolled up. That left us with the three dimensions of space and one time dimension which we live in now. If you haven't a clue what all this is about, don't worry. You need to be a physicist to understand it properly!

A Creator — a God who caused this universe to come into being — would have to exist in at least one more dimension than the universe he created. So if string theory is right and the universe began in ten dimensions, then God must live and operate in at least eleven dimensions.

This gives God unimaginable power. He would only need two dimensions of time to be able to listen to any number of people all praying to him at once. It would be no harder for him to move from one person to another in two-dimension time, listening carefully to each one, than for us to move from one film to another in the video or DVD shop, reading the labels on each one as we go.

1 trillion times greater

In fact, living in even just one dimension more than us gives God at least 1 trillion times greater power and ability than we have.

Lots of the things in the Bible that people find hard to understand or believe — things like God being three in one, or Jesus walking on water and some of his other miracles — are easily solved when we realize that God operates in more dimensions than we do.

The biggest question we are left with is not *how* God can do things that seem impossible to us, but *why* he should choose to restrict himself to our four dimensions and be born on earth as a baby at Christmas. That, as they say, is another story.

But at least now we know one thing: **Santa can't, but God can.**

Biblical index